EDUCATING
EXCEPTIONAL CHILDREN
IN REGULAR CLASSROOMS

EDUCATING
EXCEPTIONAL CHILDREN
IN REGULAR CLASSROOMS

By

HAROLD D. LOVE, Ed.D.

Head, Special Education Department
State College of Arkansas
Conway, Arkansas

CHARLES C THOMAS • PUBLISHER
Springfield • Illinois • U.S.A.

Published and Distributed Throughout the World by

CHARLES C THOMAS • PUBLISHER

BANNERSTONE HOUSE
301-327 East Lawrence Avenue, Springfield, Illinois, U.S.A.
NATCHEZ PLANTATION HOUSE
735 North Atlantic Boulevard, Fort Lauderdale, Florida, U.S.A.

With THOMAS BOOKS *careful attention is given to all details of
manufacturing and design. It is the Publisher's desire to present books
that are satisfactory as to their physical qualities and artistic possibilities
and appropriate for their particular use.* THOMAS BOOKS *will be true
to those laws of quality that assure a good name and good will.*

Printed in the United States of America
W-2

PREFACE

During the past several years an increasing cleavage has split the ranks in special education. Impetus for this split was Lloyd Dunn's article (1968) in *Exceptional Children* concerning the relevance of traditional categories of exceptionality to the problems of teaching handicapped children.

In an article appearing in *Exceptional Children* in September, 1970, M. Stephen Lilly made the statement that "traditional special education services as represented by self-contained special classes should be discontinued immediately for all but the severely impaired."

Evelyn Denos' November, 1970, Forum piece in *Exceptional Children* includes several proposals which need serious consideration, one of which follows:

> This article proposes that special education conceive of itself primarily as an instrument for facilitation of educational change and development of better means of meeting the learning needs of children who are different; and that it organize itself to do that kind of educational services job rather than organize itself as primarily a curriculum and instruction resource for clientele defined as pathologically different by categorical criteria.

Maynard C. Reynolds, in an article appearing in *Exceptional Children* in February, 1971, had this to say:

> It is a primary goal of special educators to help build accommodative capacities for exceptional children in mainstream educational programs. It is counted as a gain whenever special educators can assist regular school personnel in becoming resourceful enough to manage the education of exceptional children—either on their own or in team relationships with specialists.

This book is concerned with the cleavage that has split the special educators and also deals with the viewpoint of regular educators. Each chapter is concerned with educating a particular exceptionality in the regular classroom. In many cases the conditions must be very good for an exceptional child to function adequately in the regular classroom. This author realizes that the conditions are not always good and that special services must be provided for many children; however, we have not tried hard enough to educate exceptional children in the regular classroom. The focus of this book is directed toward that goal.

I should like to thank Mrs. Katty Crownover, Mrs. Jan Guthrie, Mr. Joe Walthall, and Sue M. Love for their help in the preparation of this manuscript. To the many authors, books, and journals who allowed me to use their material I extend my thanks.

HAROLD D. LOVE

If the individual differences of children were truly met in the regular classroom, there would be no need for various categories and labels such as educable mentally retarded, emotional disability, learning disabilities, etc. This, though, is an ideal which can never be met.

hdl

CONTENTS

EDUCATING
EXCEPTIONAL CHILDREN
IN REGULAR CLASSROOMS

Chapter 1

SPECIAL CLASSES VERSUS
REGULAR CLASSES

Dᴜʀɪɴɢ ᴛʜᴇ ʟᴀsᴛ few years an increasing cleavage has split the ranks of special educators. Dunn's article (1968) gave impetus for this division concerning the relevance of traditional categories of exceptionality as they relate to the problems of teaching exceptional children. Other articles have appeared such as Blackman's (1963) on research needs in the education of the mentally retarded. Deno's Forum piece (1970) provided a perspective that included some proposals that need serious and intensive consideration and Stephen Lilly's article (1970) "to examine present policies and practices in the field of special education and to determine the extent to which present behavior patterns in the field are educationally based and relevant to school learning and behavior problems." Books such as Roger's *Special Education* (1968) will be associated with a tendency for many educators to take a different look at what special education has been doing.

There is a significant segment of special educators which has increased its effort to maintain the status quo and in many cases has maintained its past behavior, shutting their eyes to the challenges as though they have not been raised. Many people militantly defend special education as now practiced and insist that new situations during the present need correction and that many inadequacies are not sufficient to justify not having special classes as a means for educating exceptional children. Needless to say this is a controversy.

Representatives from both sides ably present their views at conventions, in professional articles, and at symposiums. David C. Kendall made a pertinent statement in a paper delivered in

October, 1970, when he stated, "Special education is—or should be—a part of the mainstream of education, not a minor tributary with its own water conservancy board." Some educators say that special education has not been a part of the mainstream of education but has branched off into first a minor tributary and later a major tributary.

Laycock (1970) made another pertinent statement concerning not only special education but the education of all children. All educators would be wise to heed this statement: "Each child is unique in his own particular deficits, strengths and styles of learning. One of the great advances which we very greatly need to make is our ability to identify styles of learning in children."

Along this line of thinking, a quote from Lord (1970) is appropriate:

> It is much easier to explain how special education got itself out of the mainstream of education than it is to design a play to reintegrate the two programs. Some fairly obvious forces which led to the instructional separation include separate financing, the use of medical certificates for admission, the need to build up the special needs of the child in order to obtain legislation. Since it took fifty years to establish the separation as it exists today in the public schools, we may well be patient with the time it will take to significantly modify practices. It always seems to take more time to untangle a fishline than it does to acquire the tangle (p. 6).

REGULAR CLASSES

In Vermont

A fact which is very important in the education of exceptional children is that the majority of them are educated in the regular classes. Forty percent (Lucito, 1968) and 60 percent (Heller, 1968) of handicapped children do not receive adequate special education services. *McKenzie et al.* (1970) state:

> A reasonable assumption is that a sizable proportion of these children are being educated in regular classes. In Vermont, it is estimated that 80 percent of the handicapped children are in regular classes where special services are unavailable.
>
> These factors encourage the use of behavior modification procedures with handicapped children in regular classrooms. Such an

approach has been undertaken in Vermont through a program developed by the University of Vermont, the Vermont State Department of Education, and five school districts near the university. In this program, a number of elementary teachers are trained as specialists in behavior modification and its application to handicapped children. After two years of training, these specialists, called consulting teachers, serve as consultants and trainers for other teachers in their school districts.

Lord (1970) has stated that one can see that it truly is easier to explain how special education got itself out of the mainstream of education than it is to design a way to reintegrate the two programs. One of the reasons, too, that special education got out of the mainstream was that exceptional children were not being adequately cared for in the regular classes. Even today the majority of elementary school teachers do not have training in special education. Because a majority of exceptional children are educated in the regular classes, it would appear to be very important for all elementary teachers to have course work in the area of exceptional children. As Lord (1970) stated, it took at least fifty years to establish a separation as it exists today in the public schools; therefore it will take several years for the teachers in our schools and the students being educated to be trained in handling exceptional children in the regular classroom.

It does seem though that McKenzie *et al.* (1970) and the state of Vermont are going about this in the right way. They realize that the majority of handicapped children are in the regular classes in Vermont; therefore, they are training specialists called consulting teachers to serve as consultants and trainers for other teachers when helping the exceptional children in the regular classrooms.

Blatt (1970) directs several sentences toward training regular class personnel and regular supervisory people to help in the regular classroom:

> Beginning with Bennett's study in 1932, Pertsch's in 1936, this author's in 1956, and the many that followed and are being reported to this day, it has yet to be demonstrated that our existing special education models for trainable or educable children have demonstrated efficacy or special value. Further, the few studies that have

been reported concerning the education of the blind, deaf, orthopedically handicapped, disturbed, and learning disabled have not
satisfactorily demonstrated the necessity to enroll such youngsters in
currently designed special education programs. Unfortunately, however, both data and experience indicate clearly those problems
attendant with the placement of handicapped children in ordinary
school programs. Therefore, when a profession such as ours finds
itself in an unsupportable position if we turn to the right and an
equally unsupportable position if we turn to the left, we had better
find another direction to move—for, it is equally clear, that the truly
unsupportable, mindless, position is to remain exactly where we
are now. This must be a time for experimentation, and the special
training of regular class personnel and regular supervisory staff are
clearly the indicated areas that deserve of our attention.

In Other States

Considering the situation in Vermont, where 80 percent of
the handicapped children are in the regular classroom, it should
be stressed that a similar situation exists throughout the country
(see Fig. 1-1). If one breaks this down by regions one finds that
the southwest, southeast, and plains states are doing less than
other areas in the country (see Fig. 1-2). Looking at Figure 1-3,
it is noted that there were approximately 57,800,000 children
aged five through nineteen in the United States in 1968 of which
5,961,268 were reported to be handicapped. As this book is
concerned with exceptional children, it should be pointed out
that the gifted are not included in this table, and children with
learning disabilities are not included as a separate entity.

If we utilize 2 percent for the prevalence figure for gifted
children, we would add an additional 1,156,000 children to
Table 1-I which would mean that there were 7,117,000 exceptional children between the ages of five and nineteen in the
United States in 1968.

If we use a very low prevalence figure of 2 percent for
children having learning disabilities, we would add an additional
1,156,000 which would give us a total of 8,273,000 exceptional
children in the United States between the ages of five and
nineteen (see Table 1-I).

The 2 percent figure concerning the prevalence of children
with learning disabilities was used because the National Advisory

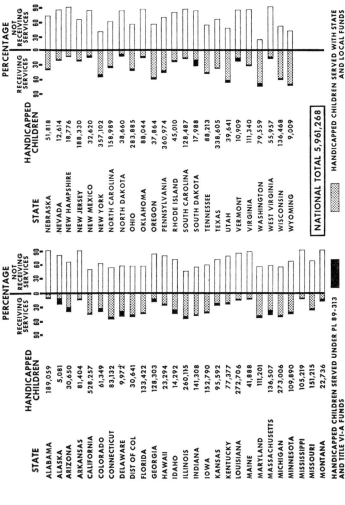

HANDICAPPED CHILDREN RECEIVING AND NOT RECEIVING SPECIAL EDUCATION SERVICES BY STATE—FISCAL YEAR 1968

STATE	HANDICAPPED CHILDREN
ALABAMA	189,059
ALASKA	5,081
ARIZONA	30,650
ARKANSAS	81,404
CALIFORNIA	528,257
COLORADO	61,349
CONNECTICUT	83,132
DELAWARE	9,972
DIST OF COL	30,641
FLORIDA	133,422
GEORGIA	128,303
HAWAII	23,294
IDAHO	14,292
ILLINOIS	260,115
INDIANA	141,308
IOWA	152,790
KANSAS	95,592
KENTUCKY	77,377
LOUISIANA	272,706
MAINE	41,888
MARYLAND	111,201
MASSACHUSETTS	136,507
MICHIGAN	273,006
MINNESOTA	109,890
MISSISSIPPI	105,219
MISSOURI	151,215
MONTANA	22,736

STATE	HANDICAPPED CHILDREN
NEBRASKA	51,818
NEVADA	12,614
NEW HAMPSHIRE	18,776
NEW JERSEY	188,330
NEW MEXICO	32,620
NEW YORK	357,102
NORTH CAROLINA	158,989
NORTH DAKOTA	38,660
OHIO	283,885
OKLAHOMA	88,044
OREGON	37,864
PENNSYLVANIA	360,974
RHODE ISLAND	45,010
SOUTH CAROLINA	128,487
SOUTH DAKOTA	17,988
TENNESSEE	88,213
TEXAS	338,605
UTAH	39,641
VERMONT	10,909
VIRGINIA	111,340
WASHINGTON	79,559
WEST VIRGINIA	55,957
WISCONSIN	136,468
WYOMING	9,009

NATIONAL TOTAL 5,961,268

■ HANDICAPPED CHILDREN SERVED UNDER PL 89-313 AND TITLE VI-A FUNDS

▨ HANDICAPPED CHILDREN SERVED WITH STATE AND LOCAL FUNDS

As reported in the 1967-1968 Title VI-A, ESEA State-wide Annual Reports on Special Education Programs.
NOTE: In 1968 there were approximately 57,800,000 children (ages 5-19) in the United States of which 5,961,268 were reported to be handicapped.

FIGURE 1-1.

HANDICAPPED CHILDREN RECEIVING AND NOT RECEIVING SPECIAL EDUCATION SERVICES (BY REGION) FISCAL YEAR 1968

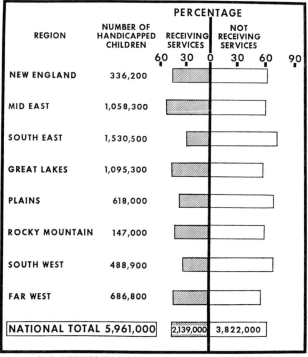

REGION	NUMBER OF HANDICAPPED CHILDREN	PERCENTAGE RECEIVING SERVICES	PERCENTAGE NOT RECEIVING SERVICES
NEW ENGLAND	336,200		
MID EAST	1,058,300		
SOUTH EAST	1,530,500		
GREAT LAKES	1,095,300		
PLAINS	618,000		
ROCKY MOUNTAIN	147,000		
SOUTH WEST	488,900		
FAR WEST	686,800		
NATIONAL TOTAL	5,961,000	2,139,000	3,822,000

As reported in the 1967-1968 Title VI-A, ESEA State-wide Annual reports on Special Education Programs.
NOTE: In 1968 there were approximately 57,800,000 children (ages 5-19) in the United States of which 5,961,268 were reported to be handicapped.

FIGURE 1-2.

TABLE 1-I

EXCEPTIONAL CHILDREN IN THE UNITED STATES

Type of Exceptionality	Number of Exceptional Children
Mentally retarded	1,503,000
Hard of hearing and deaf	286,200
Speech impaired	2,141,600
Visually handicapped	75,800
Emotionally disturbed	800,000
Crippled	305,400
Other health impaired	759,900
Multiply handicapped	89,100
Gifted	1,156,000
Learning disabilities	1,156,000
National Total	8,273,000

Estimates based on the 1967-1968 Title VI-A, ESEA State-Wide Annual Reports on Special Education Programs.

HANDICAPPED CHILDREN RECEIVING AND
NOT RECEIVING SPECIAL EDUCATION SERVICES
(BY HANDICAP)
FISCAL YEAR 1968

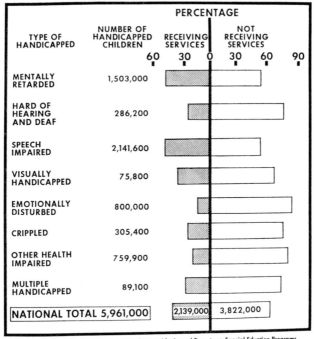

As reported in the 1967-1968 Title VI-A, ESEA State-wide Annual Reports on Special Education Programs.
NOTE: In 1968 there were approximately 57,800,000 children (ages 5-19) in the United States of which
5,961,268 were reported to be handicapped.

FIGURE 1-3.

Committee on Handicapped Children recommends that this exceptionality includes 1 to 3 percent of the school-age population.

The remaining chapters of this book will examine present policies and practices in the field of special education and determine the extent to which these behavior patterns in the field are educationally based and relevant to school learning and behavior problems. The focus of this book is on the child whose problems can be seen as relatively mild—those children traditionally labeled as educable mentally retarded, emotionally disturbed, behaviorally disordered, educationally handicapped, learning disabled, or brain injured. The one common characteristic among all these children is that they have been referred from regular classroom programs because of some sort of teacher-perceived behavioral or learning problem. The ideas presented in this book also apply to children with physical or sensory deficits, though the problem is not as immediate as with the traditional groups mentioned previously. This book will not deal with children who have been called trainable mentally retarded, severely emotionally disturbed, multiply handicapped, or with children who are so obviously handicapped that they have never been enrolled in any kind of normal school system. It should be stressed however that such children represent a small percentage of exceptional children and that the real controversy in special education is concerned with that large group of children traditionally labeled mildly handicapped.

One chapter in this book deals with the gifted. Lord (1970) states that "it is only recently that we have recognized that there are for some exceptional children, notably the gifted, several instructional approaches which have merit."

We have found that the regular classroom teacher who utilizes *enrichment* can do an excellent job in meeting the academic and social needs of gifted children. Seldom, though, is enrichment utilized properly in the regular classroom. The chapter concerning the gifted lists many valuable tips which a regular classroom teacher can utilize while enriching the educational lives of gifted children.

It is with regard to the previously mentioned exceptional children, with the exception of the gifted, that special educators have trouble justifying many practices both socially and morally and this is the area in which considerable time and energy must be spent examining both our actions and our motives.

CHANGE

Rusalem and Rusalem (1970) suggest that the timeliness of reconstructing special education is appropriate, but they state that some of the methods are unrealistic. Some critics suggest models ranging from the general reorganization of American society to modest proposals for changing the bases on which we classify exceptional children. They also state:

The "idea" people are growing increasingly shrill and pejorative in their calls for reform, and little wonder. Their exhortations on behalf of change seems to be falling on deaf ears. School year follows school year with the special education establishment retaining its structure without major modification.

Nelson and Schmidt (1971) ask several questions which they state must be answered before one can effectively deal with the efficacy problem concerning special classes. These questions follow:

1. May the constructs be used for the development of an instructional methodology?

2. Do the constructs permit the generation of statements which are reducible to operational terms?

3. Do the constructs have constitutive meaning? That is, do they permit the development of a coherent explanation of the relationship between teacher behavior and student behavior?

4. Do the constructs permit the generation of testable statements which can be used to support or modify the constructs themselves?

5. Are the constructs developed from relevant educational observations rather than from observations made in terms of some other conceptual frame of reference such as medicine or psychology?

6. If the constructs were developed from a noneducational frame of reference, can the educator make the necessary observations required to verify statements derived from them?

7. What is meant by efficaciousness (educationally speaking)? A special class is efficacious for what purpose?

8. What is a special class?

9. What instructional activities are implied when a special class is said to be operating?

10. What special class (or group of special classes) is under consideration and why this one in particular?

11. What is teaching?

These two individuals (Nelson and Schmidt, 1971) indicate that each of the above-mentioned questions is dependent for its meaning on the nature of the prior question to which it is an answer. They state that these questions must be answered before meaning can be derived from various suppositions concerning the efficaciousness of special classes. They also state:

If there is any sustaining value in the position of those who challenge or uphold the effectiveness of the special class, it must be in the systematic examination of the statements which are used to reject or justify special classes. To challenge on any other basis leads to trival conclusions.

Several special educators have indicated the need for resource teachers, clinical teachers, management specialists, or teacher aides to help regular class teachers educate exceptional children in the regular classroom. This started with Dunn's article (1968), and in 1970 special educators are still writing and adding to his original thesis. To end this chapter, the author wishes to use a statement by Haring (1970):

> Because of the lack of special education personnel, many handicapped children are served in regular classrooms. The training of resource teachers is an effective means to deal with the problem presented by these children. A resource teacher can work directly with teachers in a regular classroom to teach them methods of instruction, procedures of continuous measurement and analysis of data, and principles of behavior modification so that they may individualize instruction to suit the needs of handicapped children. The resource teacher should be trained extensively in the selection of instructional materials, the sequencing of levels of skill acquisition, the measurement of behaviors, the interpretation of data, and the management of classroom contingencies to modify behaviors.

REFERENCES

Blackman, L.: Research needs in the special education of mentally retarded. *Exceptional Children*, 29, 1963.

Blatt, Burton: Handicapped children in modal programs. *Exceptional Children in the Regular Classroom*. Special Education Training, Branch of Educational Personnel Development, U. S. Office of Education, July, 1970.

Deno, Evelyn: Special education as developmental capital (Forum piece). *Exceptional Children*, 37, 1970.

Dunn, L. M.: Special education for the mildly retarded—Is much of it justifiable? *Exceptional Children*, 35, 1968.

Haring, Norris: A strategy for the training of resource teachers for handicapped children. *Exceptional Children in the Regular Classroom*. Special Education Training, Branch of Educational Personnel Development, U. S. Office of Education, July, 1970.

Heller, H. W.: Training of professional personnel. *Exceptional Children*, 34, 1968.

Kendall, David C.: Special Education and Government. Delivered at CEC's

Northwest Regional Conference, October, 1970.

Laycock, Samuel R.: Statement to delegates attending CEC's Northwest Regional Conference, Vancouver, British Columbia, October, 1970.

Lilly, M. Stephen: Special education: a teapot in a tempest. *Exceptional Children, 37,* 1970.

Lord, F. E.: An unrealized goal of the past century—complete individualization of instruction. *Exceptional Children in Regular Classrooms.* Special Education Training, Branch of Educational Personnel Development, U. S. Office of Education, July, 1970.

Lucito, L. J.: Division of training programs—its mission. *Exceptional Children, 34,* 1968.

McKenzie, Hugh S., *et al.*: Training consulting teachers to assist elementary teachers in the management of education of handicapped children. *Exceptional Children, 37,* 1970.

Nelson, Calvin C., and Schmidt, Leo J.: The question of the efficacy of special classes. *Exceptional Children, 37,* 1971.

Roger, R.: *Special Education, Children with Learning Needs.* New York, Oxford University Press, 1968.

Rusalem, Herbert, and Rusalem, Helen: Innovative special education ideas. *Exceptional Children, 37,* 1971.

Chapter 2

THE MENTALLY RETARDED

IN THE PAST the special teacher of the educable mentally retarded has in many cases been grateful to the superintendent and/or principal for being left alone to accept the awesome responsibility of educating a handicapped child whose IQ according to law was to range between 50 and 75. Very often the IQ range of the class was between 45 and 85, and the teacher had anywhere from twelve to twenty students. In some special classes there was a conglomeration of clinical types which IQ's ranged between 25 and 50, along with the educable retardates, and also children whose IQ's approached normalcy. This, of course, is a serious mistake. It is time that superintendents, principals, and other personnel identified with regular education have it placed squarely in their laps that the education of handicapped children is their responsibility and their concern. The administrator must learn that he is not only responsible for the nonhandicapped child but that he is just as responsible for the handicapped. The principal or superintendent is just as responsible for a good program for all children as he is to his constituents for a good football program.

The people in special education have isolated themselves through the continuation of self-perpetuating interests and also because of protective attitudes of special educators. Special education should not be considered an isolated approach for handicapped children. In all probability, if individual differences were truly met in the regular classroom, there would be no need to utilize the term *educable mentally retarded.*

This chapter concerns the educational process of the educable mentally retarded child in the regular classroom. The strategies used by the regular class teacher should take care of the differences among all the children in the classroom. If the teacher truly does this, then she is doing a good job and naturally the needs of the educable mentally retarded in the regular classroom can be met and this child will not feel threatened.

Before the author goes further with this treatise concerning the educational process in the regular classroom by the regular teacher for the educable mentally retarded, it would be appropriate to quote some of the outstanding special educators concerning this controversial area.

> It is the position of this writer, based upon consideration of evidence and opinion from many and varied sources, that traditional special education services as represented by self contained special classes should be discontinued immediately for all but the severely impaired (Lilly, 1970, pp. 43-48).
>
> In a rare moment of candidness, a distinguished special educator recently remarked, during a meeting in which this writer participated, that special education isn't special nor can it, in many instances, be considered education. Studies find that, insofar as measurable abilities are concerned, mentally handicapped children in special classes are very similar in development to those in regular grades. In fact, the earlier studies of Bennett and Pertsch found that retarded children in special classes did poorly in physical, personality, and academic areas as compared with retarded children in regular classes. Later studies by Blatt and Cassidy found few significant differences between those children in the regular classes and those in special classes. Notwithstanding the many obvious and valid criticisms of studies comparing special vs. regular class membership, it has yet to be demonstrated that the special class offers a better school experience for retarded children than does regular class placement (Blatt, 1960, pp. 53-54).
>
> It is indeed paradoxical that mentally handicapped children having teachers especially trained, having more money (per capita) spent on their education, and being enrolled in classes with fewer children and a program designed to provide for their unique needs, should be accomplishing the objectives of their education at the same or at a lower level than similar mentally handicapped children who have not had these advantages and have been forced to remain in the regular grades (Johnson, 1962, p. 66).
>
> In my view, much of our past and present practices are morally and educationally wrong. We have been living at the mercy of general educators who have referred their problem children to us. And we have been generally ill prepared and ineffective in educating

these children. Let us stop being pressured into continuing and expanding a special education program that we know now to be undesirable for many of the children we are dedicated to serve (Dunn, 1968, p. 5).

Each year that a learning handicapped child is denied the services that are presently available to others, that child is being denied his right to equal educational opportunity. No argument, however well phrased, can avoid this conclusion. To the extent that failure of the Congress to act now (on the Children with Learning Disabilities Act of 1969) deprives even one child of the utilization of his learning capabilities, Congress is derelict (McCarthy, 1969, p. 35).

The above quotes from individuals would indicate that many special educators feel that we have trouble identifying our problem both socially and morally; therefore, this is the area in which we must use our time and energies examining not only our actions but also our motives.

The author now would like to write an overview of the mentally retarded, which in most books would have been at the beginning of the chapter. However, this chapter intentionally started with the controversy of where the mentally retarded should be placed, and now that the author has explained his position an analysis of mental retardation will follow.

OVERVIEW OF THE MENTALLY RETARDED

Mental retardation ranks among our most important national health, social, and economic problems. There are twice as many mentally retarded as there are cases of blindness, polio, cerebral palsy, and rheumatic heart disease combined. Only four disabling conditions have a higher incidence: cancer, arthritis, cardiac disease, and mental illness. (See Table 2-I).

Each person varies in his ability to learn, to adapt, to develop to his maximum capacity and to live a useful, satisfying life in our society. The mentally retarded are those children and adults who, as a result of inadequately developed intelligence, are significantly impaired in these abilities. Within this definition is found a broad range of persons—from those with a profound handicap to those with only a slight impairment. The challenging fact is, however, that regardless of the degree of retardation,

TABLE 2-I

ESTIMATED INCIDENCE OF MENTAL RETARDATION IN
UNITED STATES BY DEGREE OF SEVERITY

| | DEGREE OF RETARDATION | | | | |
	Profound	*Severe*	*Moderate*	*Mild*	*Combined*
Approximate IQ level	0-19	20-35	36-52	53-80	
Estimated number of retarded	85,000	200,000	350,000	5.4 million	6 million
Percent of all retarded	1½%	3½%	6%	89%	100%
Incidence of total population	1 person/ 1000		3 persons/ 1000	26 persons/ 1000	30 persons/ 1000

it is possible to help the retarded develop and live more useful and satisfying lives.

Only a few years ago it was thought that nearly all the mentally retarded should be placed in residential institutions. In recent years the philosophy on treatment of mental retardation has changed. Currently, fewer than 5 percent of the estimated six million mentally retarded individuals in the United States live in institutions. The remaining 95 percent live in local communities.

Most experts now agree that the local community is the best place for treatment and training. This places even greater emphasis on the responsibility of communities and counties to provide the necessary programs and facilities.

Many communities have begun to recognize this responsibility. People from all walks of life have begun to show an increasing awareness and concern about mental retardation. In numerous communities individual people, organizations, and private agencies have voluntarily initiated programs to help the mentally retarded. They have recognized the public's responsibility. This increasing public awareness and concern has also led to enabling legislation and has placed some responsibilities related to mental retardation with government departments and agencies at all levels: national, state, and local. However, in almost all of these programs the major responsibility for analyzing local needs and planning and implementing programs to meet these needs rests with the local people.

What Causes Mental Retardation?

There are over five hundred known or suspected causes of mental retardation. Here are several causes that are perhaps the most familiar:

1. Prematurity.
2. Chromosome abnormalities such as mongolism.
3. Inborn metabolism errors such as PKU (phenylketonuria).
4. Rh-factor incompatibility between mother and infant.
5. Brain injuries at birth.
6. Childhood infectious diseases (such as measles) severe enough to cause inflammation of the brain.
7. Excessive x-ray during early pregnancy.
8. Virus diseases such as German measles in the mother during the first three months of pregnancy.
9. Heredity.
10. Socioeconomic factors.

Yet, according to most professional opinion, all five hundred of the known or suspected diseases and conditions account for less than 25 percent of all the cases of retardation. In over 75 percent of the cases, the specific cause has not been isolated.

In many retarded individuals no known organic brain damage can be found. Their retardation is apparently due to socio-cultural factors and other causes. Among the mildly retarded there are many neglected children. These children are born with normal intelligence but become retarded only because they are neglected and because they exist in a home and neighborhood environment where their physical, educational, and emotional needs are neglected.

Mental development, like physical development, is promoted by the right kind of activity and stimulation. Mental development is retarded when the right kind of activity and stimulation is lacking. The years of early childhood are of critical importance when the nervous system is maturing and language developing.

The severely retarded or trainable child is likely to have organic defects. Severely retarded children tend to be distributed relatively evenly throughout all sections, income groups, and classes in our society. The mildly or educable retarded, however, generally do not have physical handicaps which identify them as being mentally retarded. These children frequently are the product of an environment in which there is a lack of learning, a lack of developmental opportunities, and a lack of intellectual stimulation.

History

Mental retardation was one of the earliest limitations to be recognized in the public schools. Special classes were first organized in this country in 1896, and by the end of the first two decades of the twentieth century, 222 special classes were to be found in the larger cities of the United States. It has been recognized for many years that this condition affects 2 to 4 percent of the school-age population, but it was only around 1960 that the needs of this group of children received nationwide attention.

The treatment of the mentally retarded has been a sad chapter in the history of mankind. In the savage tribes in the early years of civilization, the low-grade mentally retarded were often cast out to perish as being unworthy members of the human race. It is also known that the Spartans left the mentally retarded to their fate in the cold weather or else bashed their heads against a rock. This ruthless destroying of these unfortunate people by the Spartans was done, they rationalized, in order that their nation would not degenerate. The rise of Christianity saw a spirit of sympathy being shown for the mentally retarded.

During the Reformation period of European history, there was much persecution of the mentally retarded. Many people who could not understand the teaching of Catholicism or of Protestantism were ruthlessly persecuted.

There was no attempt made to educate mentally retarded children until 1799. A wild boy was found living with dogs in the forest of Aveyron in southern France. He was diagnosed as an idiot, but Jean Marc Itard decided that he could educate the boy using a systematic sensory training system. Itard worked patiently with the wild boy for five years, but he made little progress and was forced to give up when the boy became unmanageable at the onset of puberty.

In 1937 a pupil of Itard's, Edward Seguin, founded a school in Paris for the mentally retarded. Seguin, as a teacher and medical student under Itard, had become very interested in educating the mentally retarded. He published a book in 1864 entitled, *The Moral Treatment, Hygiene, and Education of Idiots, and Other Backward Children.* Seguin is best known for physiological methods for treating the mentally retarded and in 1866 wrote his second book in which he described these methods and stated reasons why he believed in their worth in educating the retarded child. The physiological methods consisted of "adaptations of the principles of physiology, through the development of the dynamic, receptive, reflexive, and spontaneous functions of youth" (Seguin, 1866).

Seguin taught that the teacher must first educate the muscular system of the child. This education must be done through certain activities, and Seguin believed that activities must be those which satisfy the child's own needs, desires, and capacities. He also believed that exercises would strengthen any part of the body that happened to be weak. Seguin advocated that along with the muscular exercises, the teacher must also provide sensory exercises. The most important senses to be trained, according to Seguin, were tactile, auditory, and visual. Recognizing that speech was the most difficult skill for the mentally retarded to acquire, he taught speech, writing, and lastly reading.

In 1897, Dr. Maria Montessori became interested in educating the mentally retarded. She studied the works of Itard and Seguin and came to the conclusion that the problem of mental retardation was essentially a pedagogical one rather than a medical one. Montessori not only began educating the mentally retarded at the psychiatric clinic where she worked and at various asylums in Rome, but also began training teachers of the mentally retarded. She was the first person to greatly emphasize the importance of training good, well-qualified teachers in the field of special education.

Montessori believed in auto-education or self-teaching and used didactic materials to train all the senses except taste and smell. She organized the materials and activities in such a way that the children taught themselves while the teacher withdrew into the background.

Massachusetts opened the first school for mentally retarded children in America in 1850 and named it the Massachusetts School for Idiotic and Feeble-Minded Youth. Later the name was changed to the Walter E. Fernald State School at Waverly. Providence, Rhode Island, established the first classes for the mentally retarded in the public schools in 1896, and Springfield, Massachusetts, established classes in 1897. Many other cities followed shortly thereafter but the bulk of the mentally retarded children remained in the regular classroom and were frustrated, denied an adequate education, and usually dropped out of school at the first opportunity.

The early public school special classes for the mentally retarded included those with a wide range of ability from the severely retarded to those bordering on dull normal intelligence. The advent of the intelligence test paved the way for the differentiation of those who could achieve academic learning from those who could profit from self-care activities.

The first classes used a "watered down" approach which covered the same materials and subjects that were covered in the regular classroom. The mentally retarded children were just given a watered down version of the same materials and the teacher used a longer period of time to cover these materials. There was much drill and rote learning. Unfortunately, this is still a much-used approach to teaching the mentally retarded.

It is interesting to note that most of the major contributors to the education of the mentally retarded during the nineteenth century were physicians, with the exception of Alfred Binet, a psychologist. During the early history of the education of the mentally retarded, educators were willing to let medical men take the responsibility for the methods and materials used in education. It is also interesting to note that education was aimed primarily at sense and muscle training, and the means used most often were didactic or self-teaching devices. Some of these methods are still in vogue today.

Since 1950, the growth of special classes for retarded children has been remarkable. Even in the five-year period from 1953 to 1958, the increase in enrollment was 260 percent, an amount larger than for any other area of exceptionality. This growth has resulted primarily from the demands and pressure of parents of these children.

Prior to the special class movement for mentally retarded children, such boys and girls were usually excluded from public schools by school laws or regulations because they were uneducable. Parents were expected to care for them at home or place them in an institution. Contending that they were taxpayers and that their children were capable of learning, the parents banded together and charged that the schools had the same responsibility to retarded children as to all other children.

A national organization, now known as the National Association for Retarded Children, was established by groups of parents about 1950. One of the chief aims of this organization and its state and local chapters was to foster public services for trainable retarded children. Parents carried their demands to state legislatures and, as a result, legislation authorizing local public school systems to establish special classes for this group was passed in many of the states. Despite the tremendous strides which have taken place in special programs for instruction of the mentally retarded, only one half of the nation's 25,000 school districts offer classes for pupils having special learning problems and needs.

In the field of mental retardation, as in practically no other, organizations of parents have been influential all over the world. Much help has been provided by organizations which dedicate themselves to generating public interest in and increasing understanding of the mentally retarded and their needs.

Local parent organizations began to appear as early as 1930 because of a serious need to further the welfare of retarded children, their families, and friends. The first national organization established in the United States, the National Association for Retarded Children, was formed by a few parents and a number of professional persons and interested citizens who saw the need to bring the tremendous problem of mental retardation to public attention.

The establishment of this organization signaled the beginning of a major development for retarded children. Its great strength and impact on the field of mental retardation has resulted in more legislation, funds, research, and services for the intellectually handicapped. By 1968 its membership had grown to more than 60,000 persons, state federations had been formed in forty-eight states, and over seven hundred local parent groups had been organized.

In many communities, local chapters of the NARC and private citizens' organizations have been instrumental in establishing nursery schools, day care centers, preschool classes, special classes in public schools, schools for trainable children, day camps, residential camps, sheltered workshops, recreation programs, occupational training centers, social group programs, and programs of public education. The local chapters have established parent guidance and group therapy programs which have proved valuable in offering moral support to parents faced with either the influence of a retarded child at home or their guilt feelings at having placed their child in an institution. Through lectures and other materials made available by the national office of NARC, parents may obtain a general understanding of the meaning of mental retardation, their needs, and the impact of a retarded child in the family.

The NARC has done much to make the nation aware of the extent and causes of mental retardation, rid parents of shame and ignorance, and develop improved programs of care, treatment, and rehabilitation of the retarded in the communities as well as in institutions. It has worked diligently to acquaint citizens and agencies of the community with their responsibilities to the mentally retarded. It has also undertaken a program of research aimed at discovering the causes of mental retardation and developing preventive measures.

In 1962, NARC was the recipient of one of the first awards presented by the Joseph P. Kennedy, Jr., Foundation for outstanding work in the field of mental retardation. The organization was commended for awakening the nation to the problems of mental retardation and for proving that the retarded can be helped.

The National Rehabilitation Association and United Cerebral Palsy Association are two other national organizations which deal with problems involving mental retardation, and they have contributed to the growth of services that the mentally retarded and their families need.

One of the best-known professional organizations concerned with the field of mental retardation is the American Association of Mental Deficiency, of which Edward Seguin served as first president. Since its inception in 1876, this organization has had a long history of notable scientific contributions toward helping the mentally retarded. Representatives of institutions devoted to the care and education of the retarded first assembled in Philadelphia to discuss questions relating to the causes, conditions, and statistics of retardation, and to the management, training, and education of mentally retarded children. However, most reports of the AAMD never reached the public, the potential for improving understanding going unnoticed for years.

The AAMD has membership from the fields of medicine, psychology, education, and social work, and publishes the *American Journal of Mental Deficiency.* It has made progress in the professional area where much enlightenment is taking place and new interests are being generated, leading to new answers for treatment, training, and prevention.

Another professional organization, the Council for Exceptional Children, had its inception in 1922. The function of this organization is to bring together special educators of the United States and Canada in areas of exceptionality. In 1941 it became a department of the National Education Association, and by 1968 its membership had grown to over 25,000. Through its publications and various state and local chapters, it has been a constant stimulus for improvement and enrichment of public school programs for the mentally retarded.

Our late President, John F. Kennedy, gave the world a new concept of mental retardation. He dignified the words "retarded child" and challenged all of us to continue the work he had set in motion, which included projects designed for prevention of mental retardation and services for those for whom prevention discoveries will come too late.

Appointed by Kennedy in 1961, a panel of twenty-seven leaders in science, education, and other professions made the first thorough survey of what was being done for the retarded and what needed to be done. Its comprehensive recommendations, which reflected the public's concern with the problem of mental retardation, resulted in legislation providing for improved research, prevention, professional training, and services for the mentally retarded.

After Kennedy's famous message: "We have too long neglected the mentally retarded," many developments occurred in rapid succession—a Special Assistant on Mental Retardation was appointed by the President; a White House Conference on Mental Retardation was called; Congress passed major legislation in planning, manpower, prevention, and construction; the Department of Health, Education, and Welfare assumed the responsibility for implementation; and universities, professional organizations, and parent associations accelerated their efforts on behalf of the retarded.

Prior to John F. Kennedy's significant contributions to the betterment of the mentally retarded, increased emphasis on the equality of educational opportunities had already turned our attention toward improving the education of all handicapped children. But even though programs for handicapped children in the public schools had been subsidized by an increasing amount of legislation, the shortage of qualified teachers and personnel made it difficult for public schools to establish or expand special programs.

The federal government first acted to alleviate this teacher and personnel shortage in 1958 when Congress passed Public Law 85-926, which, as amended in 1959, authorized an appropriation of one million dollars a year to assist institutions of higher learning and state education agencies in the training of leadership personnel in the education of the mentally retarded. In 1963, Public Law 88-164 was signed into law, expanding the provision of Public Law 85-926 to authorize assistance in the preparation of professional personnel in all areas of the handicapped, including children who are mentally retarded, deaf, speech and hearing impaired, visually handicapped, seriously emotionally disturbed, and crippled.

The amended law makes grants available for the preparation of persons employed or desiring to be employed as teachers of the mentally retarded, instructors in colleges and universities preparing teachers of the mentally retarded, supervisors and administrators of special education programs, speech pathologists, audiologists, and other specialists. The five basic types of grants available are undergraduate traineeships for college juniors and seniors, graduate fellowships for both the master's and post-master's levels, summer-session traineeships, special-study institutes, and program-development grants.

The last decade has seen an historic emergence of mental retardation and the mentally retarded child from isolation and public indifference. Many factors have contributed to this development, such as major federal involvement in programs for the retarded, a reawakening in the states to their own service needs, and a national information campaign by public and private agencies to build public awareness and understanding of mental retardation and the mentally retarded. As developments such as these and research into the causes, treatment, and prevention of mental retardation continue to be made for the welfare of the six million retarded persons in the United States today, history will continue to be made.

Education of the Retarded

The author would like to reiterate at this point a statement made previously in this chapter: If teachers truly take care of individual differences in the classroom, to which we give so much lip service in education, there would be no need for the term *educable mentally retarded*. It is a known fact that a child having an IQ of approximately 50 to 75 is usually diagnosed as educable mentally retarded when he enters first grade, and after he leaves school this diagnosis no longer is valid or at least people do not know that the individual is retarded. It appears then that an individual is diagnosed as mentally retarded from about the age of six through eighteen. After that he melts into society and loses the tag of retardation. The tag, though, has taken its toll and the damage on the person's personality and ego has been done.

One of the major causes of social maladjustment in mentally retarded children is lack of educational achievement. Many special educators feel that adequate social adjustment does not take place in a special class designed for fifteen or eighteen educable mentally retarded children.

It should be pointed out that in this chapter the author is not talking about the child having an IQ below 50 or the multi-handicapped child having disabilities so apparent that he must be placed in a special class in order for attention to be given to his obvious needs. It is a fact, though, that most educable mentally retarded individuals function more like normal people than they do like subnormal people.

There is a great deal of controversy concerning placement of trainable mentally retarded children in the elementary school as opposed to a day care center away from the regular elementary school. This chapter does not propose to enter into this argument, but the author does state that the trainable retarded child needs special attention in a special class and should not be integrated into the regular classroom. At the same time the author takes the view that most educable mentally retardates having IQ's between 55 and 75 can be adequately educated in the regular classroom.

In considering the possibility of educating the educable mentally retarded in the regular classroom, the following quotation from the President's Committee on Mental Retardation appears to be pertinent:

> We now have what may be called a 6-hour retarded child— retarded from 9 to 3, five days a week, solely on the basis of an IQ score, without regard to his adaptive behavior, which may be exceptionally adaptive to the situation and community in which he lives (1969).

If all the children in the regular classroom are given the same basal reader, then, of course, the mentally retarded child will not be properly instructed in reading. If all children in the elementary grades are given the same worksheets, the same arithmetic books, and the same type of instruction, then the mentally retarded child will not have a chance in such an environment. But if these things are done in the regular classroom, then the gifted child, the bright normal, and in all probability the slow learner and the average will not be cared for properly.

A mentally retarded child must be given work in the regular classroom at his instructional level. The teacher must give him attention and also utilize gifted students to help some of the retarded ones.

Homework

The mentally retarded child in the regular classroom or special class will probably not benefit from homework. Actually, if a teacher takes care of individual differences when she assigns homework, then if she has thirty students in the classroom she must give thirty assignments in homework. If the gifted child is challenged in the homework assignment, of course the rest of the children miss the challenge. If the average child is challenged, naturally the slow learner, the retarded, the bright normal, and the gifted child are not challenged. If the mentally retarded child is challenged by the homework, then of course all the other children having IQ's above 75 will not get a great deal of meaning from the homework. Many parents say that homework instills good study habits in their children, but the fact remains that the parent and the home situation are responsible for instilling study habits and seldom does homework help in this area.

The teacher of regular classroom children must take courses in special education if she is to handle exceptional children in the regular classroom. In most colleges across the country we educate teachers and yet they are not exposed to any of the areas of exceptionality which they will find in their classroom. Instruction that they get in the education courses generally deals with the normal and above average child and seldom deals with the child having problems or with the mentally retarded child. This must change if we are to get the full benefit from the taxpayer's money in educating all children to the utmost of their ability.

Grades

For a mentally retarded child to function in the regular classroom we are going to have to stop giving the grade of "F" to elementary children. It would be a good idea not to give this grade at all. One of the most devastating things a child can do is to take a report card home with "F's" on it and be faced with giving this report card to his parents, the people whom he respects most. Very few children have ever been helped by being given a grade of "F"; thousands and thousands have been hurt considerably by being awarded a grade of "F."

Repeating Grades

Seldom does it help a retarded child or a slow learning child (IQ 75 to 90) to repeat a grade. Research indicates that academically the child does little better the second year than the first year. While it seldom helps, it almost always leaves devastating scars on a child's personality. There are no easy answers to repeating grades or awarding the grade of "D" and "F." At the same time, if we would open our eyes to the fact that we are scarring the personalities of children irreparably by doing these two things, we could not in good conscience as educators continue to do them.

Psychological Examinations

During the past several years psychological tests have been indiscriminately given to too many children. There is no real reason to test an entire class of students if they appear to be doing well. The only reason that psychological examinations are in order is to determine a specific disability or to utilize a score as a tool in the remedial process. Therefore it is recommended that psychological examinations not be given to young children before the age of six unless they are suspected of being trainable or profound retardates or having multiple handicaps.

Too often when a child has entered school the teacher has a score and this score becomes a brand; thus the teacher expects the child to act as he has been stereotyped. Many educators call this the self-fulfilling prophesy. In other words a teacher is told that a child is mentally retarded; therefore she treats him like a mentally retarded person and thus he acts and becomes in essence a mentally retarded person. Our IQ scores have gone a long way in helping to propagate and perpetuate this self-fulfilling prophesy. It is hoped that, in the future in the early-childhood education programs, mass psychological testing is not done and these tests are given only on a referral basis or in just a few cases when a mental age might possibly be of help. In all probability few teachers have ever been told a child's IQ score when that teacher could not determine from classroom performance a very good educated guess as to the child's true score. This score, though, or number, or brand, or tag has done a great deal in crippling and scarring the personalities of many children. Again, it should be repeated that if individual differences are met in the regular classroom, there will be no place for terms such as *slow learner, educable mentally retarded, immaturity,* and the like which brand a child as being inferior. There is no real reason to compare all children with a norm.

The Little Red Schoolhouse

Perhaps in the 1970's we can go back a few years and borrow a few of the good things about the one-room school. During the days when we had one-room schools, we moved children ahead, we kept them at their various levels, without its being extremely traumatic for the child and in many cases for the parents. In many of the one-room schools report cards were not needed and in essence were not required. Why not borrow a few of the good things from the one-room school as we go down through the years castigating this fading part of the scene in America? There were some good things about the one-room schools. The above-mentioned things are paramount, and these are the things which we have lost in the school systems today.

Reading

In the school systems of America we often say that 40 to 50 percent of the children have a reading deficiency at various grade levels. It would appear that if that many children have reading deficiencies then there is a great deal wrong not only with the teaching methods but the materials from which we teach. There is a possibility that the basal reader, however important it is, is just a tool and should be utilized as a single tool in a classroom along with many other tools to insure that a child is reading properly. One of the most important skills that a child will ever develop is reading. Naturally, if he is thrown in above his head at the beginning and continues at a rate above his head, he will never read effectively. We tend to do this with the basal readers and with all teacher-made worksheets which are utilized in the elementary schools. To sum up reading in the entire educational process, we keep coming back to two words, "individual differences." The individual differences of thirty children having IQ's ranging from 55 to 150 can be met in a regular classroom. It is not an easy task but teaching is not supposed to be an easy task.

In discussing his blueprint for change, Dunn (1968) mentions what he labels, "A Thought." Dunn's thought is pertinent to this chapter:

> There is an important difference between regular educators talking us into trying to remediate or live with the learning difficulties of pupils with which they haven't been able to deal; versus striving to evolve a special education program that is either developmental in nature, wherein we assume responsibility for the total education of more severely handicapped children from an early age, or is supportive in nature, wherein general education would continue to have central responsibility for the vast majority of the children with mild learning disabilities—with us serving as resource teachers in devising effective prescriptions and in tutoring such pupils.

Teacher Aids

In speaking to school administrators concerning teacher aids, we learn that superintendents and school board members generally feel that the teacher-aid program is too expensive. Because of this feeling, the teacher-aid program has not been given a chance in our educational process. Concerning finances for the very important teacher-aid program, the following quote from the President's Committee on Mental Retardation should sum up the feeling of all educators: "We have got to stop talking as if money is not available. It is. It is about time that the educators of the country begin to name the priorities" (1969).

Homogeneous Grouping

Dunn (1968) indicates the following:

> Homogenous groupings tend to work to the disadvantage of the slow learners and underprivileged. Apparently such pupils learn much from being in the same class with children from white middle class homes. Also, teachers seem to concentrate on the slower children to bring them up to standard.

In the Judge J. Skelly Wright decision in the District of Columbia concerning the track system, it was ordered that tracks be abolished. It was contended that tracks discriminate against the racially and/or socially and economically disadvantaged and were therefore in violation of the Fifth Amendment of the Constitution of the United States. Passow (1967), after conducting a study of tracking in the D. C. school system, reached the same decision concerning tracking.

Since special classes, special schools, and grouping in the regular classrooms are forms of homogenous grouping and tracking, what are the implications of Judge Wright's ruling for special educators? President Nixon's Committee on Education recently ruled that homogenous grouping in the regular classroom discriminates against minority groups and/or socially and economically disadvantaged children. Dunn (1968) answers the question for special educators:

> What if the Supreme Court ruled against tracks, and all self-contained special classes across the nation which serve primarily ethnically and/or economically disadvantaged children were forced to close down? Make no mistake—this could happen! If I were a Negro from the slums or a disadvantaged parent who had heard of the Judge Wright decision and knew what I know now about special classes for the educable mentally retarded, other things

being equal, I would then go to court before allowing the schools to label my child as "mentally retarded" and place him in a "self-contained special school or class." Thus there is the real possibility that additional court actions will be forthcoming.

Several eminent special educators have recently made statements concerning educating exceptional children in the regular classrooms. A few of the statements follow:

> Except for the moderately to severely handicapped, the instructional problems of most exceptional children are not distinctly different from those of normal children. It is difficult or impossible to identify a learning principle and/or teaching guideline which is uniquely applicable to such exceptional children. It is a well known fact that teachers of normal children often copy the drill devices and teaching aids which special teachers have worked out in desperation. There seems to be only one "type" of nervous system which is stimulated by a set of somewhat similar receptors (Lord, 1970, p. 7).

> The philosophy behind diagnostic/prescriptive teaching is in close agreement with much in Dr. Lilly's article. We believe strongly that the majority of children who have traditionally been found "mildly handicapped" should be kept in the mainstream of education rather than stigmatized with labels and isolated in special classes. We have found that when teachers seek help for children whom they perceive as posing academic and/or behavioral problems, they want practical information from a behavioral point of view. In other words, they want to know exactly how to teach the child. In the past, they have not gotten this information. The child has been categorized with a psychomedical label by his performance on standardized tests and placed in a class on this basis. This tells the teacher nothing about the kind of learning environment the child needs, what motivates him, his particular academic and social strengths and weaknesses, or how to program for them. If the teacher received information of this kind, and was helped to put it into practice, there would be far less need for special classes; the regular teacher would be able to reach the child before the "problem" ever got out of hand (Reilly, 1970).

In a reply to a review of his book, Rappaport (1970) had this to say concerning special classes:

> In keeping with this principle, the intent of the book was not to be regarded as a panacea to all educational ills. Its intent was only to provide one route away from the conventional special class, which too often has been and still is a deplorable dumping ground, overseen

by an inadequately trained teacher and initiated because the school board was pressured into doing "something" to a special class that will in fact meet the needs of its children (p. 9). Moreover the book advocates that to meet those needs adequately, the goal must be to have a program that will enable most children with learning disorders to overcome their deficits sufficiently to return to regular classes where they then can learn successfully.

It would appear that even when a child needs an educational environment other than a regular classroom, he is harmed by psychomedical categorizing labels which are totally unnecessary. If a child is placed in a special class we must study the child's entire educational milieu. Only then can we place the child appropriately.

REFERENCES

Blatt, B.: Some persistently recurring assumptions concerning the mentally subnormal. *Training School Bulletin, 57,* 1960.

Dunn, L. M.: Special education for the mildly retarded—Is much of it justifiable? *Exceptional Children, 35,* 1968.

Johnson, G. O.: Special education for the mentally retarded—a paradox. *Exceptional Children, 29,* 1962.

Lilly, M. Stephen: Special education: a teapot in a tempest. *Exceptional Children, 37,* 1970.

Lord, F. E.: An unrealized goal of the past century: complete individualization of instruction. *Exceptional Children in the Regular Classroom.* Special Education Training, Branch of Educational Personnel Development, U. S. Office of Education, July, 1970.

McCarthy, J. M.: Testimony. *Hearings Before the General Subcommittee on Education.* Committee on Education and Labor. U. S. Government Printing Office, 1969.

Passow, A. H.: *A Summary of Findings and Recommendations of a Study of the Washington, D. C. Schools.* New York, Teachers College, Columbia University, 1967.

President's Committee on Mental Retardation. A Report on a Conference on Problems of Education of Children in the Inner City. The six-hour retarded child. Warrenton, Virginia, Airle House, 1969.

Rappaport, Sheldon: In An Author's Comment. *Exceptional Children, 37,* 1970.

Reilly, Vera Vinogradoff: Letters to the Editor. *Exceptional Children, 37,* 1970.

Seguin, Edward: *Idiocy and Its Treatment by the Physiological Method.* Albany, Brandon Printing Company, 1866. Reprinted, New York, Teachers College, Columbia University, 1907.

Chapter 3

THE GIFTED CHILD IN THE REGULAR CLASSROOM

Over the years the gifted child has been educated in the regular classroom probably more so than any other exceptional child. Research indicates that in most cases they have not worked up to mental capacity. The chief reason for this is because they do the work assigned them, make good grades, and the work does not go far enough to challenge them.

During the 1960's, interest in the education of gifted children in the United States was intensified even more than in the 1950's. This interest is not new; throughout the centuries attempts have been made in various cultures to identify and educate the gifted.

In the sixteenth century, Suleiman the Magnificent, the Ottoman sultan, established a system of selecting the gifted youth throughout the Turkish Empire. His scouts went in search of the fairest, strongest, and most intelligent Christian youths in the population. The children were educated in the Mohammedan faith, science, religion, art, and war. "In ancient Greece, over 2000 years ago, Plato advocated that children with superior intellect be selected at an early age and offered a specialized form of instruction in science, philosophy, and metaphysics" (Kirk, 1962).

As late as the 1930's there was a great amount of apathy concerning the gifted in the United States. Goetsch (1940) presented evidence that 90 percent of the superior high school graduates who came from the upper-income groups were able to go to college, but less than 20 percent of superior high school graduates from the lower-income families were able to attend college. According to Goetsch, Americans were providing higher education only for the gifted who were economically able.

In 1957 the launching of two Russian space satellites produced a clamor for technicians and scientists. "These incidents sharpened concerns which had been developing for more than a decade. A struggle for scientific and technological leadership began in earnest during and following World War II" (Freehill, 1961).

Military events accelerated the need for intellectual competence and America began to expand its educational program shortly after 1957. We have found that the scientist plays a vital role in military strategy.

The G.I. Bill has provided the opportunity for a college education to many individuals who otherwise could not afford to go to college. The National Science Foundation and the National Defense Education Act support science majors, and many scholarships and fellowships are now available to college students.

IDENTIFICATION

In studying the gifted, there has been a major problem of agreement among educators as to just what is the definition of gifted. The term *gifted* has many meanings to many people. There is no such thing as an accurate composite of a gifted child (Abraham, 1958). However, there are devices and named characteristics by which the gifted can be identified.

There is a belief that a teacher is an excellent judge of gifted students in his class. Despite all assets a teacher could have for making a proper identification, only limited agreement is found between giftedness as judged by a teacher and giftedness as measured by standardized tests (Pegnato and Birch, 1959).

Even with limitations, teacher judgment can supplement other identification tools. To become more effective, each teacher should become better acquainted with signposts of giftedness as described by Durr (1964): "The gifted student is likely to have: above-average language development; persistence in attacking difficult mental tasks; the ability to generalize and see relationships; unusual curiosity; a wide variety of deep interests."

Because of emotional involvement, parents either overestimate or underestimate the abilities of their child according to signs of giftedness. Parents can answer questions concerning the child that are impossible to other observers. For example:

1. Does he have a mature vocabulary?
2. Does he understand and use complex sentences?
3. Does he have a retentive memory?
4. Does he show unusual interest in number relationships?
5. Does he demonstrate an interest in books at an early age?
6. Does he have a wide variety of interests?
7. Does he evidence an eagerness to learn?

These questions lead one to suspect giftedness, but an affirmative answer does not always denote this trait. It should also be pointed out that a child can be gifted without possessing all of these characteristics.

In order to adequately detect superior children, the schools must have a systematic program for screening to detect giftedness.

It is stated by Dehaan that a good identification program should discover other characteristics besides a child's aptitudes and capacities. It should discover interest, motivation, personality, and social factors (Dehaan, 1957). The final result should not be in the identification of all these traits, but should be to place each child into the educational situation most suited to develop his capacities.

The intelligence quotient, which shows the relationship of mental and chronological age, has long been, and is today, the primary standard of finding the gifted student. Even with this single factor, there is a wide difference of opinion as to the beginning of giftedness. This criterion could allow giftedness to begin at 115 IQ or as high as 180 IQ. The intelligence test can be administered to a group, but more accurate results are obtained when it is administered individually. According to Abraham, the intelligence test helps to determine a child's general capacity but does not indicate in which direction his giftedness or mental limitations reach, nor does it necessarily show his capacity for various academic areas (1958).

Buhler and Guirl (1960) state that existing intelligence tests are not always an adequate identification of the gifted and have developed a checklist for identifying the more able student. The student is to be rated on a scale proceeding from Low, 2, 3, 4, or High. They are rated on thirteen specific aspects which are as follows:

1. High academic achievement.
2. Advanced vocabulary and reading level.
3. Expressive fine arts talent.
4. Wholesome personal-social adjustment.
5. Early physical competence.
6. Superior intellectual ability.
7. Effective work independently.
8. Persistent curiosity.
9. Strong creative and inventive power.
10. Special scientific ability.
11. High energy level.
12. Demonstrated leadership abilities.
13. Well-developed mechanical skills.

Another school screening device for detecting giftedness is the achievement test. This test measures the amount of learning that has occurred in subjects covered in school. They have been given to representative samplings throughout the nation and scores of any single child can be interpreted and compared according to the nation's norms. There are many strengths and weaknesses of this test as an identification means. The strengths are due to the construction and standardization of the tests and the comparable forms which allow for reevaluation. According to Durr (1964), the limitations are several:

> These tests indicate only the levels of achievement that students have actually attained, not allowing for the underachievers; lower achievement might be the result of lack of materials and facilities for study as in lower socio-economic homes, or inadequate teaching of any area; no provision is made for curriculum differences. Again, research has revealed that one method should not dictate the identification procedure, but rather should complement it.

It is stated by Dehaan (1957) that some studies have revealed the definition of "gifted" to include those talents in the "fine arts." Abilities in the fine arts are difficult to measure but can be identified by a method which combines some features of standardized tests and some aspects of personal observations. A sample of the child's work is obtained and rated by a panel of expert judges. This method has been used to discover children with abilities in art, creative writing, music, dramatics, and mechanical skills.

Abraham (1958) and Dehaan (1957) recognize still another means of identification—that of relationship in the peer group. Because they have intimate contacts quite removed from the classroom, children can provide information that is ordinarily unavailable to the teacher. Sociometric techniques point to leadership, intellectual ability, mechanical, and physical aptitude.

Goldberg (1958) states that the creative child has often been misplaced in society. Since most standardized tests have omitted the factor of creativity, many gifted in this aspect have been overlooked. When we use conventional identification procedures only, young people able to produce novelty in the learning process as well as remembrance of course content will be missed.

The gifted child has all the fundamental needs of childhood: comfort, affection, exercise, play, security, self-respect, rest, and so forth. One should be both subjective and objective in attempting to identify gifted children. Examples of both methods are listed below:

Subjective	*Objective*
Observation	Readiness tests
School marks	Mental ability tests
Work samples	Achievement tests
Interest inventories	Aptitude tests
Interviews	Personality tests
Rating scales	
Autobiography	
Sociometry	

Teachers and educators must identify and adequately provide for America's gifted children. Witty (1957) tells us that America is in a struggle to determine by which goals and ideals the people of the world will live, and needs talented men and women equipped through education to find solutions to problems old and new. The gifted can best provide resourcefulness and imagination necessary to create a better world.

Case Studies of the Gifted

Case 1

John Stuart Mill, the son of an English author and philosopher, is estimated to have had an IQ above 190. He began studying Greek at the age of three, Plato at seven, and Latin at eight. At the age of nine, Mill was studying Newton's arithmetic as well as geometry and algebra.

When he was twenty years old, John Stuart Mill experienced mental illness. He realized that he had become a reasoning machine and turned to music and poetry for therapy. This superior insight helped him develop his emotional life, and it was surprising to most people that he could so adjust himself.

James Mill, John's father, treated him like an adult, but kept him out of school and away from other boys. James educated his son at home.

The history and accomplishments of Mill raise an important question: Do we need the formal school situation for the education of the highly gifted?

Case 2

For all of his eighty-three years, Karl Witte was well adjusted and intellectually bright. His IQ is estimated to have been above 180. Before the age of eight, he was reading Italian, French, Greek, and Latin. Although Karl received his Ph.D. before he was fourteen, he was still considered to be extremely normal.

Case 3

Norbert Weiner had great difficulty learning by rote and did counting in elementary school on his fingers. Yet he was known for his theories of cybernetics from which digital computers have been developed. Norbert graduated from high school at the age of eleven and obtained his Ph.D. in mathematics at the age of eighteen. But with a rigid lockstep approach, the school system would not allow him to enter school before the age of six, saying he was too immature.

The education and early history of Einstein, Pasteur, Darwin, Churchill, and Newton differ markedly from the early history of Mill, Witte, and Weiner. The former share, in retrospect, a reputation for poor school achievement. The difficulties encountered by these men were those of interest and not lack of ability. These cases are the exceptions. Typically, gifted children do extremely well in school.

A CORNUCOPIA OF INFORMATION

Previous research, some of which is classical, current enlarged research, and increased development of diagnostic instruments have made significant contributions to the techniques, methods, and procedures of inquiry used in dealing with problems of the maladjusted gifted. A hasty sampling of the research tends to broaden the teacher-counselor's purview and make more effective the necessary interpersonal relationships with gifted children.

The following is a brief catalogue of some of the research:

1. The basic and classical studies of Terman and Oden (1951) touch on just about every aspect of the gifted child's life. Terman and Oden reported these data: (a) the gifted child is slightly a better physical specimen, (b) he is healthier, (c) he is accelerated in grade placement, (d) he is not equally as high in all school subjects, (e) he learns to read quite early and he likes to read, (f) he has many hobbies, (g) his knowledge of play and games is two to three years advanced, (h) he grows up to be well adjusted, and (i) he tends to marry someone with high mental ability.

2. Drews' study (1961) in Lansing, Michigan, found that professionals and managerial families gave a high proportionate share of gifted children to the total gifted population.

3. Werblo (1966) says that gifted children have a tendency to under-evaluate their abilities.

4. Barbe (1963) found that gifted youngsters produce to the fullest extent only when they are happy in their tasks.

5. Barbe (1963) also found that the gifted respond to socialization pressures and accept adult values readily. They generally have good work habits and are highly competitive.

6. The Portland Five-Year Study (1966) recorded that tools such as artwork, autobiographies, and compositions reveal information concerning self-concepts, teacher-pupil concepts, adult concepts, and information about communication.

7. Martinson (1962) indicated that properly enriched educational programs often show the needs, drives, desires, and counseling areas for the gifted population.

These data demonstrate a tremendous source of material available to the teacher. Perhaps many or all of the items noted above are truisms to the observant and knowledgeable teacher of the gifted. However, all concerned personnel should be cognizant of the increasing body of information in the field and they should at least attempt a familiarization.

Do the Gifted Have Personality Problems?

The writer has chosen the following as an operable definition of personality: "Personality is the sum total of an individual's internal and external patterns of adjustment to life" (American Psychiatric Association, 1964).

Gifted children do have personality problems, the same as average and below-average children do. However, consulted research evidences that the percentage of the total gifted population afflicted with personality problems is considerably lower than the percentage given for problem children in the total child population.

The talented child does acquire problems, and if he does not receive attention and guidance the problems may become intensified. Writers and scholars seem to have rejected the popular conceptions of the gifted child as "queer," "impractical," "freakish," and "maladaptive." The gifted child is generally pictured by authoritative writers as being healthy, emotionally stable, and likeable. Outwardly, gifted children appear to be much like other children. Maladjustment problems are usually combinations of adult misunderstanding, underachievement, unfulfilled social, personal, and status drives, and poor self-concepts.

Knowing the Child's Abilities

Parents often ask, "How can I help my gifted child?" One answer is to know his capacities so that you can make reasonable demands of him. The mother of a gifted five-year-old said to the child's teacher:

Since you told me that my child was mature, more like a seven-year-old, I have experimented with giving him more responsibility and more freedom of choice. He now does simple errands for me, takes care of his clothes better, helps other children and seems happier than formerly. He gets into mischief less because he is proud of his new duties and takes the responsibilities seriously. Temper tantrums and negative behavior have virtually disappeared.

Parental Attitudes Toward the Bright Child

In handling a bright child, parents seem to be attracted to one of two extremes: they either neglect or belittle him, laugh at what strikes them as absurd in the child's behavior, and fail to understand why he is different from other children; or they exploit his exceptional traits at every turn and push him beyond normal limits.

Possibly parents do not realize the extent to which they identify with their gifted child, finding in the child's precocity compensation for their lack of education or intellectual achievement. As a teacher of a gifted class once put it at a parents' meeting, "These parents think they're the gifted children."

Most parents seem aware of spectacular talents rather than high intelligence in their children, and they often think of these talents as God-given or inherited, if not wholly inexplicable. Many parents cling to the older notion that a gifted child is doomed to become a neurotic and a failure. Parents seldom are the best judges of their children's aptitudes and talents in comparison with other children because they are not sufficiently acquainted with the range of abilities in the age-group population of their children.

Parents as Teachers of Gifted Children

Parents are inevitably teachers and counselors; the first and the strongest influences on a child are those of his parents and the home environment. A child's home background will largely determine the course of his development. In many cases the guidance and training of wise parents have offset the disadvantages of poor schooling and a meager environment.

The childhood of people who developed unusual creative

talent suggests that the bright and talented flourish in homes where parents encourage original thinking, questioning, and experimentation without being too demanding. The mother's influence is great, but studies show that the father's influence can be an even stronger force in shaping a child's intellectual tastes and interests.

Congenial family living fosters sound emotional and social development in children and in the case of the gifted, normal family life can forestall traits such as onesidedness, bossiness, selfishness, or solitariness. A gifted child of sixteen has this to say about parental influences: "The thing that helps most is not coercion or great concern about school marks, but the creation of an atmosphere that greatly develops one's special abilities."

The Home

It is well established that the intellectual atmosphere of the home and the influence of the parents play a large role in the early years of childhood, which prompts many to ask the following question: "Why aren't parents of young gifted children given suggestions concerning the way to make their influence count even more?" Probably, the best answer to this is that if we must tell the parents about the young gifted child without the parents recognizing him spontaneously, then the suggestions would not be of great value. However, this does not mean that parents should not be given suggestions concerning how to deal with their gifted child.

Those parents who show off their precocious child often make him obnoxious to others. To say the least, it is poor taste for parents to brag constantly about the child's accomplishments or to exploit the gifted child's many talents. The gifted child does best if his parents treat him as a normal member of the family but encourage him in every way, and he avoids the "genius complex" and playing up their egos by showing off his superiority. The child does best when he is allowed to be himself—when he is allowed to play with normal children and to make wholesome contacts with people in the community. The parents should never satisfy their unfulfilled needs and desires by exploiting the child, thereby making themselves feel that their life is being fulfilled by something that the child does.

The Disadvantaged Gifted Children

Research and classroom observations indicate that devaluation of education is widespread among children from economically and culturally disadvantaged environments. Poor study habits and motivations appear to be a common result of these environmental circumstances. Gifted pupils from this segment of the population tend to display an aspiration level much lower than their academic potential. These pupils also tend to achieve at a level much lower than gifted pupils from the upper socioeconomical stratum.

A special school in Kentucky, the Lincoln School, operated by the University of Kentucky College of Education, has been established as a new approach to the education of these children and also as a research center to study their peculiar learning problems. The curriculum at the Lincoln School is determined by the academic needs of the individual students, and the curricular innovations are studied in conjunction with the habits of the students and the research needed. The preliminary data gathered by the Lincoln School showed a potential for success in training these children. There is also much value in the research observations that will come from this school.

Education

There are still many elementary schools which have no administrative provisions for the gifted. If the teacher is given a free hand in the development of curriculum materials and if an atmosphere of creativity is developed in the regular classroom, there need be no administrative provisions for the gifted. Educational opportunities should not be denied the gifted child because groups delay action in the belief that equal educational opportunities should be interpreted to mean the same provisions for all students. No student in a given classroom has the same educational opportunity. The teacher determines the educational opportunities for each child in a given classroom.

The following pages will discuss the various approaches to educating the gifted child. The approach which is talked about the most but practiced the least is enrichment. As one reads about enrichment, he can plainly see that if this approach is given an equal opportunity or at least if it is practiced in the regular classroom, then it is probably the best approach for the gifted child. Again we go back to individual differences being cared for in the regular classroom, because it is an inescapable fact that if we do not care for individual differences in the classroom, then of course not only will the gifted not be challenged, but also the other children will not be challenged.

Problem Areas

There is no doubt that we will find some children who are so bright that they cannot be cared for in the regular classroom. These represent a very few of the entire gifted population. Many of these children will go on to college when they are ten, eleven, and twelve years of age. Because they represent such a small number of the entire gifted population, they will not be discussed in great detail in this chapter. During the past few years there have been four different cases which have made the national headlines because of their extreme giftedness. All of these children have entered college at a very early age and at this writing all four have done extremely well. The author realizes that there are probably many more cases involved than just these four, but as stated previously these were prominent in the national newspapers.

Ability Groupings

Some of the school programs have instigated ability groupings for individual courses or they generally follow the multi-track approach. Ability groupings, though, discriminate against the child from the low socioeconomic level and also discriminate against children having low intelligence. This type of approach also discriminates against the minority groups, because invariably they are all placed in the same group. No matter how we try to get around ability grouping, the fact remains that we discriminate against the very children that we say we are trying to help when we break them into ability groupings.

The best place for a group of children having IQ's ranging from 60 to 150 is in the regular classroom. There should be about eighteen to twenty-two of these children per teacher and if possible with a teacher aid. The teacher who is willing to work and who has the knowledge concerning the various exceptionalities can take care of all the individual differences in each classroom. Each child can be challenged, and each child can be instructed at his level. It is not easy to do, and it is very difficult for continued practice. But as stated already, it can be done and should be done.

Although many educational methods have been tried, education for the gifted continues slowly and sporadically. A program for the gifted child should include two types of giftedness—intellectual and talented. Other basic principles that should be included in an educational program are as follows:

1. To develop an open mind.
2. To develop leadership abilities.
3. To disregard competition and materialism in the program.
4. To be more realistic.
5. To provide for many kinds and types of motivational drives, learning rates, and creative impulses.

But more important, this educational program should be flexible and should enrich the lives of the students. If it fails to accomplish these two objectives, too many of our gifted children will fail to contribute greatly to the development of our society. A gifted child's strengths and gifts will largely individualize his program so that he will have longer and larger blocks of time for his specialities. The educational goals that we list for the gifted are very similar to those we desire for all youngsters. The difference will be in their ability to exercise leadership, the quality of performance, and the quantity of the learning experience.

The kind of program adopted in a given school system is determined by the philosophy of education held by the administration, teachers, and parents. The other important factors are the facilities and materials available, the size and geographical distribution of the school population, and the school and community personnel that can be utilized.

According to one author, both Shakespeare and Gertrude Stein used punch lines which can help us to understand some of the educational terms so lightly used in the study of gifted children. These lines are, "What's in a name?" and "a rose is a rose is a rose" (Abraham, 1958).

Some of the most popular ways of educating the gifted child are enrichment, acceleration, skipping grades, segregated classes, partial segregation, separate schools, itinerant teacher—the list is intriguingly long.

Although much controversy surrounds the method of acceleration, this is still one of the most common ways of dealing with the gifted child. There is no evidence that groups of children are handicapped by acceleration. Research agrees in general that children profit academically from acceleration if it is not carried to an extreme. It also encourages the belief that acceleration in moderation (a year or two) does not have an adverse affect on the social and emotional development of children. However, many people are familiar with individual cases where acceleration had appeared to be detrimental.

Acceleration, any procedure which enables a student to complete a year or more earlier than the norm for his age, was one of the first methods tried in bringing closer together the abilities of gifted students and the programs of the school. The usual procedures in acceleration are as follows:

1. Admission to school according to mental age.
2. Skipping a grade.
3. Early admission to college.
4. Telescoping (covering material in shorter period of time).

Enrichment is another technique for educating the gifted. This is a means of providing learning activities over and above that provided for the average child in the regular classroom.

The itinerant teacher program is sometimes used in working with gifted children. This program usually represents a compromise between placing gifted children in a modified special class and keeping them in the regular classrooms. The itinerant teacher acts as a consultant to the regular teacher in special areas and meets a few hours a week with special groups of gifted children in certain subject matter fields.

Teachers of the Gifted

If parents listen to their children or watch their behavior, they soon realize that the teacher is the most important out-of-home influence in a child's life. Many leaders and eminent persons remark that good teachers are in large measure responsible for their exceptional achievements. All teaching is creative, and teachers utilize basic materials which, in this case, are the minds and aspirations of young children.

One of the best articles concerning successful teachers of the gifted is by Bishop (1968). Some of the conclusions from his research follow:

1. Teachers who were judged effective by intellectually gifted, high-achieving students did not differ with respect to teachers not so identified, relative to such variables as sex, marital status, type of undergraduate institution attended, highest degree held, course work preparation, and extent of association with professional organizations.

2. Successful teachers of gifted students tended to be mature, experienced teachers.

3. Teachers who were successful with mentally superior students were mentally superior themselves. They stood in the upper 3 percent, relative to the general adult population, and significantly higher than their teaching colleagues.

4. The effective teachers tended to pursue avocational interests which were "intellectual" in nature. They had a significantly greater interest than their teaching colleagues in literature and the arts, and in the cultural life of their community.

5. The identified teachers were characterized by high achievement needs—they attempted to do their best and to succeed. This was reflected in past scholastic achievement as well as present teaching success.

6. Teachers identified as effective by gifted students supported special educational provisions for gifted students. A significantly greater percentage of them preferred to teach a class of exceptionally bright students than did their fellow teachers.

Opinions of Gifted Students

Parents and teachers often determine what is best for the gifted student without consulting the youngster concerning what he thinks is best for himself. A group of students in San Diego were interviewed to obtain their recommendations for academic program changes (Rice and Banks, 1967). Generally, these students preferred the following:

1. More freedom in course selection and more emphasis upon a general education philosophy.

2. French, German, humanities, creative writing, general mathematics, chemistry, physics, psychology, and economics courses.

3. More intellectual criticism and discussion of controversial issues.

4. More recognition for their work.

5. Some type of selective academic segregation. It is suggested that other school districts conduct similar interviews to aid them in program planning.

According to the above-mentioned research, if gifted students were given freedom to redesign their own curriculum, they would do the following:

1. Demand more freedom in course selection.

2. Eliminate many of the physical education courses (boys and girls), home economics classes (girls), and shop courses (boys).

3. Place more emphasis upon literature, drama, art, and music.

4. Endorse the general education philosophy, yet make provisions for individual specialization by interest area.

5. Add more social sciences to the curriculum (early junior high school students differed significantly from the rest of the group by scorning social studies).

Gifted Underachievers

One of the dilemmas, precipitated by parents, which continues to command the attention of educators concerns the pressuring for maximum academic performance of children classified as underachievers. In the case of intellectually gifted children, many investigators have concluded that adequate adjustment is positively correlated with high achievements. With the advent of instruments to make possible the identification of creative children, Wonderly and Fleming (1965) investigated the creative child who is an underachiever. These two researchers concluded:

> On the assumption that intelligent, creative children, who are doing less well than their peers in school achievement may be considered to be in anxiety provoking situations, the hypothesis that they will demonstrate their awareness of the presence of frustration by being less well adjusted than their achieving neighbors was tested.
>
> The results suggested that underachieving, intelligent, creative children were no better or less well adjusted than achieving, intelligent, creative children. This indicates that in spite of their being subjected to criticism by parents and teachers for not performing as well as they might, there was no evidence of personal dissatisfaction or depressed self-concept, as demonstrated by the self-rating scale, and no loss of status or acceptance by peers, as demonstrated on the peer-rating scale.
>
> It may be that creative individuals do call on their unique talent in times of emotional stress, but apparently such stress is not generated by situations which would normally be considered threatening. There is obviously a need for research in the area of frustration tolerance for creatives.

We live in a complex, changing world; therefore it is not a matter of chance that we see a growing emphasis upon creativity at this time. It is necessary that the schools provide children not only with information of the present and the past, but also with the opportunity for innovation and change. Parents, too, should help provide the children with information, understanding, societal values, and with capacities for innovation and change.

In all cases, it appears that progress comes primarily through creative activities. One of the really striking things to come from recent research on creativity is the relationship between cognitive processes and variables such as interest, attitudes, personality, and background. The research indicates that high creatives tend to seek unusual vocations, and they follow their own interests rather than those of the teacher. The same research indicates that they have an unusually high sense of humor and exhibit stable tendencies to holistic, analytic, and inferential perception and thinking.

Terman Studies

Scientific thought on the nature and nurture of intelligence is tremendously indebted to Lewis E. Terman, late professor at Stanford University. He directed the revisions of the Stanford-Binet Intelligence tests and contributed in untold ways to the identification of ability.

> Terman's doctoral thesis, dated 1907, compared the learnings of seven bright and seven dull children. He followed this in 1913 with a study of bright children in San Francisco. In this study he found, that, contrary to public opinion, the children were not sickly, queer, or anti-social. Another study of 124 children in 1919 was a forerunner of the tremendous work that is usually known as the Stanford Studies of Genius. These investigations were begun in 1921 with money secured from the Commonwealth Foundation. To this Terman added other grants and some money from his own university. With these funds he assembled a staff which included such currently famous names as Burks, Oden, Cox, Goodenough, Kelley, Ruch, Willoughby, and Yates (Freehill, 1961).

In 1920 Terman identified 1,528 gifted children and followed the group for thirty-five years, until his death in 1956. During these years he was instrumental in writing five books entitled *Genetic Studies of Genius* (Terman, 1925-1959).

The selection of Terman's subjects was based on an IQ of 140 and above on the 1916 Stanford-Binet Intelligence Test. The ratio of boys to girls was 116 to 100; there were 100 percent more Jewish children than in the general population and fewer Italian, Mexican, Negro, and Portuguese children than in the general population.

The group included about 50 percent in professional occupations and less than 7 percent in unskilled or semiskilled work.

The mean number of grades completed by the fathers and mothers was twelve, four grades more than the average of that generation. One third of the fathers and 15 percent of the mothers had graduated from college.

As a whole, the group remained highly superior intellectually and most stayed in the top 1 to 2 percent of the school population. School achievement was in line with that of intelligence. The quality of work for the group, generally, was exceedingly high.

It was found that gifted children who had been promoted more rapidly than is customary were equal as a group or superior to gifted children who had progressed in the customary manner. Furthermore, these subjects showed better adjustments in health and work, continued their education further, and were more successful in their careers.

The educational attainments of the gifted were far above the norm for all people. It was found that the gifted were concentrated at the upper levels of vocational achievement.

The gifted produced gifted children. The gifted subjects' offspring had a mean IQ score of 132.

On the whole, the gifted were physically superior to the unselected population. At birth they averaged three quarters of a pound heavier than average. They learned to walk and talk earlier. At the average age of forty-four years their mortality rate was four-fifths that of the general population.

It was found that educationally the typical gifted child accelerated in grade placement 14 percent of his age, but in mastery of his school subjects, he was accelerated at 44 percent of his age. Ninety percent of the men and 86 percent of the women attended college. Seventy percent of the men and 67 percent of the women graduated.

The gifted were less prone to make overstatements and to cheat. They were above average on an emotional stability test, and after twenty years of being studied 80 percent showed satisfactory adjustment, 15 percent had some maladjustment, and 5 percent had serious maladjustment. There was less alcoholism among the gifted than the average population, and the divorce rate was less than for the general population. Although it is too soon for the trends of Terman's study to be definite, it would appear that the gifted are happier than the general population in marriage, have fewer divorces, are better adjusted, and have fewer offspring.

Several other longitudinal studies corroborate the Terman findings and add additional ammunition to the belief of many educators that "gifted people support the world, the rest of us are hangers-on." The world enjoys the fruits of the bright person's labor.

Range of Interests

Gifted children usually exhibit a greater range of interests than do average children. One of the most consistently recorded leisure-time activities for the gifted is reading. It appears that they read a greater quantity of material and the list of topics is much broader than for the general population. Hobbies of the gifted include the collection of stamps, insects, rocks, etc. The collections of the gifted usually are more extensive and show much better organization than those of the general population. Even though gifted children are prone to occupy themselves with interests that require intellectual powers, they also participate in games played by their peers.

The occupational aspirations of the gifted usually involve the professions and semiprofessions, particularly law, medicine, college teaching, and banking.

High Creative Versus High IQ

Probably the most extensive report of comparisons across the two groups (H_cL_{IQ} and L_cH_{IQ}) was research done by Getzels and Jackson (1958). In spite of a twenty-three-point difference in IQ scores the two groups achieved equally well. When the teachers were asked to rate the students on the degree to which they enjoyed having pupils in class, the high IQ group was much more desired than the creative group. The difference in desirability was investigated by asking both groups of students to rate the personal traits of moral character, creativity, goal directedness, emotional stability, and sense of humor. They ranked these traits with a number of sets: (1) the extent to which they wished to be high on the trait, (2) the degree to which high performance on the traits would lead to success in later life, and (3) the extent to which they thought teachers would prefer these traits. The most important difference between the two groups concerning the eight personal traits was that of sense of humor. This was ranked high by the creative group and last by the IQ group. Concerning the perception of the qualities needed for success as an adult and those preferred by teachers, both groups had the same. Although the above is true, the high creative pupils did not want for themselves the traits perceived as leading to success or favored by the teacher. The high IQ students, though, wanted for themselves the traits they perceived would lead to success and also be favored by the teachers.

In analyzing verbal and nonverbal drawings in relationship to imaginative productions, it was found that the creative groups seemed to want to please themselves with the productions rather than please other people. Concerning occupational goals the creative group chose fewer conventional professions such as doctor or lawyer and chose more unconventional ones such as inventor and writer.

Some Attempts at Definition

The following are some of the attempts that have been made to define the gifted child:

The academically talented student is one who receives scores of about 115 or over on a Stanford-Binet Intelligence Test or falls above a similar point on one of the Wechsler Intelligence Scales (American Psychology and Guidance Association, 1961).

The gifted is one who has a high order of ability to handle ideas, to produce creatively, and to demonstrate social leadership (Educational Policies Commission, 1950).

The talented child is a pupil with an especially high potential in one or more general or specific areas, whose potential cannot be adequately developed without special provision with the curricular, extra-curricular, and counseling programs (Fair).

The gifted child is at least a child of high intelligence. (Anything more than that we do not know, and with anything more we are at present not vitally concerned.) (Goddard, 1928.)

The gifted is in the top one percent of the juvenile population in general intelligence (Hollingworth, 1942).

The gifted child is one who makes very high scores on general intelligence tests (Nason, 1958).

The gifted is one whose performance in a potentially valuable line of human activity is consistently remarkable (Witty, 1951).

National Trends Concerning the Gifted

In recent years a number of nationwide trends have developed with regard to the gifted:

1. An increased (extra-school) awareness of the potential contributions of the gifted.

2. A growing curiosity as to just what giftedness is.

3. An increase in graduate research on the gifted and their problems.

4. A growing awareness on the part of educators of the importance of making special educational provisions for the gifted.

5. An increase in the number of state departments of education which are making educational provisions for the gifted.

6. An increase in the number of publications on the gifted.

7. An endorsement of the ungraded and enrichment-type program for the gifted in the elementary schools.

8. A greater acceptance of ability grouping in regular classes for the gifted in the secondary schools.

9. An increase in the number of training programs for teachers who are interested in teaching the gifted.

10. An increase in the number of guides on programs for the gifted for teachers and administrators.

11. The introduction of college courses in the high school programs for the gifted.

12. A growing acceptance of the term gifted to designate the "intellectually superior."

13. A growing acceptance among the schools of defining giftedness on the basis of a percentage of the student population of a school.

14. The recent determination to make able students work harder, take more years of solid subjects, and spend less time in nonacademic pursuits.

15. Greater concern with identifying and creating programs for the gifted from the lower socioeconomic groups.

16. An increase in funds to train teachers of the gifted and for fellowships for students from the U. S. Department of Health, Education, and Welfare.

17. A growing realization that giftedness consists of many intangible qualities and intelligence is just one of them.

Issues

The following are only a few of the crucial issues concerning the gifted that deserve serious discussion:

1. What constitutes giftedness or even mental superiority?

2. How does the gifted react toward the groups in which he happens to be?

3. How do the varying groups react to the gifted?

4. What are the operant personality traits, such as tenacity, initiative, and motivational patterns, of the gifted?

5. In many states determination of the responsibility for the gifted hasn't been made.

6. What content and methodology will make the best program for the gifted children?

Influences

There have been many influences at work on our country's response to the gifted:

1. World War II heightened society's sensitivity to its need to benefit more fully from the superior potentials of the gifted.

2. The launching of the first Russian satellite in October, 1957.

3. The almost hysterical concern about our educational system by the public.

4. The constructive suggestions of the timely and perceptive Rockefeller report on the "Pursuit of Excellence," the Conant report, and the Rickover report.

5. Interested figures (nationally recognized persons) in our society have caused people to be aware of the problem by displaying interest in the gifted.

6. Influence of professional and industrial persons in recognizing and helping the gifted.

7. Favorable results demonstrated by existing programs for the gifted.

8. Our interpretations of the term "democracy" have retarded the growth of programs for the gifted.

9. Demands of our culture for scientists and mathematicians have caused more children to be guided into these fields.

10. The oversupply of scientists and the unemployment rate among them during the early 1970's.

Problems of the Gifted

Teachers should be acquainted with the common problems as well as the attributes of gifted children. Gifted children do have special problems, but they share some of the problems of normal children.

One of these problems that is most puzzling to teachers is underachievement. This term applies to children whose school achievement does not measure up to their high potential. The dynamics of underachievement are complex. It may stem from fear of failure, a desire for independence or security, or an expression of hostility, anxiety, or inner conflict (Strang, 1963, p. 498). Other possible causes are personal illness or illness in the child's family, or other family difficulties such as divorce or financial problems (Issacs, 1962, p. 498). Poor teaching, poor study habits, lack of student effort, or absorbing nonacademic interests such as swimming, painting, or reading may also be at fault.

What can the teacher do about underachievement? First, he should develop a sane attitude toward the problem. A child should not be tagged lazy or shiftless just because he is lagging in academic work. Second, the teacher should reevaluate his attitude toward the underachiever. Why should he be concerned if the student enjoys school life and does not seem overly concerned about the poor quality of his work? The teacher should consider the quality of his instruction. Is he getting his explanations across to the student? Third, the teacher should consider counseling with the student. Bright children are more capable of critical appraisal than others of the same age (Hildreth, 1966, p. 433). They should consider the following questions: Is this the best I can do? If not, why not? Do I want to improve? If so, what can I do to improve? Perhaps this conversation will give the teacher some insight into why the child is underachieving. Fourth, the teacher should not forget that one way to deal with the underachiever is to accept him as he is so long as no serious failure is impending. This means permitting him to choose his own pace and tolerating the interests his maturing mind seems to dictate. "Underachievement may be a temporary condition that will disappear with fresh stimulation from one source or another" (Hildreth, 1966, p. 433).

Many techniques are helpful for the teacher who wishes to individualize instruction for the gifted. No one technique is better than another. No writer can outline a program of instruction for a teacher. But a brief discussion of techniques which should be explored include small-group work, independent study, unit teaching, group independent study, and the discovery method of teaching. Other opportunities for enrichment such as work on school publications, out-of-school projects and activities, and the gifted as teachers for other students should be explored.

The tool subjects—reading, writing, arithmetic, and spelling—can be taught so that each student can work on his achievement level. The class is divided into small groups for each of these subjects. Although a small range of skill mastery should be permitted in each group, the members are not necessarily functioning at the same level. Grouping should be flexible so that the "red-birds" are not always identified as the fast group, the "blue-birds" as the slower one. Many resource materials are required for small-group instruction. A second grade student capable of mastering fourth grade material should have a fourth grade book. However, care should be taken that this is not the same book which is standard equipment in the fourth grade classroom.

Various activities can be assigned to similar small groups. A small group might compile a dictionary of slang to share with the class. A study might be made of old slang terms. What has happened to them? How many have stayed in the language; how many have become outdated?

Gifted students might be allowed time for independent study of problems related to their specific interests. The child with an electronics hobby might construct a simple telephone. The boy or girl ornithologist could investigate the physics of bird flight. These studies should be shared with the class.

Many challenging activities might grow out of unit teaching. In this method total class work is organized as a broad learning unit that grows out of the interests and needs of the class.

Teachers should not neglect the discovery method of teaching. Hildreth aptly applies an old Chinese proverb, "Those who can think learn for themselves and not from the sages" (Hildreth, 1966, p. 224). Students should be required to seek information independently and use it in problem solving.

Finally, teachers should not overlook work on school publications, out-of-school and community libraries, auto instructional materials, and the use of the gifted as instructors for other students as means of enrichment. School-wide projects and activities—the annual, the newspaper, assembly programs, and so forth—are suitable outlets for the gifted child's originality and creativity.

An imaginative teacher can think of many more activities to individualize instruction for the gifted. It should be remembered, however, that individual instruction for bright students can only succeed as part of an individual program for all pupils. The teacher who is sincerely interested in providing such a program should be as well informed about all her students as she is about the gifted.

REFERENCES

Abraham, Willard: *Common Sense About Gifted Children.* New York, Harper and Brothers, 1958.

American Psychology and Guidance Association. *Guidance for the Academically Talented Student.* National Education Association, 1961.

Barbe, Walter: Occupational adjustments of the mentally gifted. In Crow, Lester D., and Crow, Alice (Eds.): *Educating the Academically Able:*

A Book of Readings. New York, McKay, 1963.

Bishop, William E.: Successful teachers of the gifted. *Exceptional Children,* 34, 1965.

Buhler, Ernest O., and Guirl, Eugene N.: The more able student: described and rated. *Vocational Guidance Quarterly,* Summer, 1960.

Committee of Public Information: Psychiatric Glossary. Washington, American Psychiatric Association, 1964.

Dehaan, Robert F.: Identifying gifted children. *School Review,* 65, 1957.

Drews, Elizabeth M., *et al.*: *Guidance for the Academically Talented Student.* National Education Association Project on the Academically Talented Student and American Personnel and Guidance Association. U. S. Government Printing Office, 1961.

Durr, William K.: *The Gifted Student.* New York, Oxford University Press, 1964.

Educational Policies Commission: *Education of the Gifted.* National Education Association, 1950.

Fair, Jean: Excerpts from a recent report on Evanston township high school talented youth program. Talented Youth Committee, Evanston Township High School, Evanston, Illinois.

Freehill, Maurice F.: *Gifted Children, Their Psychology and Education.* New York, Macmillan, 1961.

Getzels, J. W., and Jackson, P. W.: The meaning of giftedness: an examination of an expanding concept. *Phi Delta Kappan,* 40, 1958.

Goddard, Henry Herbert: *School Training of Gifted Children.* Chicago, World Book Company, 1928.

Goetsch, Helen B.: Parental income and college opportunities. *Teachers College Contributions to Education, No. 795.* New York, Teachers College, Columbia University, 1940.

Goldberg, Miriam L.: Research on the gifted. *The Teachers College Record,* 40, 1958.

Hildreth, G.: *Introduction to the Gifted.* New York, McGraw-Hill, 1966.

Hollingworth, Leta S.: *Children Above 180 IQ.* Chicago, World Book Company, 1942.

Isaacs, A. F.: Survey of research on the gifted. In Trapp, P., and Himelstein, P. (Eds.): *The Exceptional Child: Research and Theory.* New York, Appleton-Century-Crofts, 1962.

Kirk, S. A.: *Educating Exceptional Children.* Boston, Houghton Mifflin, 1962.

Martinson, Ruth A., *et al.*: *Special Programs for Gifted Pupils.* Sacramento, California, State Department of Education, 1962.

Nason, Leslie J.: *Academic Achievement of Gifted High School Students.* Los Angeles, University of Southern California Press, 1958.

Pegnato, Carl W., and Jack W. Birch: Locating gifted children in junior high school: a comparison of methods. *Exceptional Children,* 25, 1959.

Rice, Joseph P., and Banks, George: Opinions of gifted students regarding secondary school programs. *Exceptional Child, 34,* 1967.

Strang, R.: Psychology of gifted children and youth. In Cruickshank, W. M. (Ed.): *Psychology of Exceptional Children and Youth.* Englewood Cliffs, N. J., Prentice-Hall, 1963.

Terman, Lewis M. (Ed.): *Genetic Studies of Genius.* Stanford, Stanford University Press, 1925-1959, Vols. I-V.

Terman, Lewis M., and Oden, Melita H.: The Stanford studies of the gifted. In Witty, Paul (Ed.): *The Gifted Child.* Boston, D. C. Heath, 1951.

Werblo, Dorothy: Experiences in historical research and changes in self evaluation of gifted children. *Exceptional Child, 33,* 1966.

Witty, Paul: Current practices in educating the gifted child. *Educational Monograph,* Fall, 1957.

Witty, Paul: *The Gifted Child.* D. C. Heath and Company, 1951.

Wonderly, Donald M., and Fleming, Elyse S.: Underachievement and the intelligent creative child. *Exceptional Child, 34,* 1965.

Chapter 4

THE PARTIALLY SIGHTED CHILD

Most educators agree that institutional placement for a handicapped child is the last resort. If at all possible, children should remain with their parents and attend school in the community where they live. This chapter deals with the child who has a vision problem which is not severe enough to indicate institutional placement. He may be partially sighted or legally blind but nevertheless can be educated in the regular classroom.

DEFINITION

The incidence of mild visual defect is fairly high. It is estimated that about one out of every four children has some type of vision problem. However, recent studies indicate that a small proportion, approximately one in four hundred of the preschool and school population, have such marked visual difficulties that even with the best medical and optical care they cannot see well enough to profit by the educational facilities that are provided for children with normal vision. Kerby (1952) found that less than 30 percent of 7,310 children in partially sighted classes actually fell between 20/70 and 20/200 after correction. This leads one to believe that the lower limit of vision for educational purposes is indeed difficult to define. According to Hathaway's revised book, the following children should be classified as partially seeing:

> Children having a visual acuity of 20/70 or less in the better eye after correction. Correction means that all necessary medical and surgical treatment has been given and compensating lenses provided when needed. Such children, must, however, have a residue of sight that makes it possible to use this as the chief avenue of approach to the brain.

Children with a visual deviation from the normal who, in the opinion of the eye specialist, can benefit from the special education facilities provided for the partially seeing. Special educational opportunities for children after eye operations, if readaptation in eye use and psychological readjustment is required, and for those with muscle anomalies, such as strabismus, which demand re-education of an eye and psychological readjustment (Hathaway, 1959, p. 16).

IDENTIFICATION

Early examinations, beginning at preschool age, are the best way of identifying partially seeing children. Vision examinations should be continued at intervals throughout the individual's life.

Eye examinations for the preschool child should be relatively simple. A child three or four will have difficulty in following directions, particularly if the directions become too involved. Young children may be asked to identify familiar objects that have been placed at varying distances. Fink (1954) suggests that familiar objects may be drawn on a circular card and the card rotated at different angles. The child is asked to identify the object using one eye, then the other, and finally both eyes are tested together.

For testing children of school age, three types of examinations will be described: (1) Snellen, Telebinocular, Ortho-Rater, and Massachusetts screening tests, (2) informal observation by parents and teacher, and (3) examinations by eye specialists.

An intensive research study of methods of screening school children for visual defects was made in St. Louis in 1948-49. The results of this study showed that of six vision screening tests, the Snellen and Massachusetts Vision tests were very practical for school use (Foote, 1954). The Telebinocular and Ortho-Rater are considered by many to be excellent screening tests, especially for upper elementary school children.

The test for visual acuity is considered the most important test of visual ability. The Snellen test is used for this purpose because it utilizes a chart designed with test objects, symbols or numbers of graded sizes, drawn to a definite scale. It must be given correctly to be of value. Cleanliness of the chart, proper lighting of the room, and placement of the child at the correct distance from the chart are very important if the results are to be reliable. It is suggested that, if possible, the teacher or school nurse give this test. The teacher knows her pupils and can judge whether they are in a proper physical or emotional condition to take the test. The teacher can also note significant eye symptoms by observing the children at work and play. The school nurse who usually works very closely with the teacher may also give the test and rely on the teacher for observation and valuable hints which can lead to the detection of eye problems. The Snellen Chart can detect such conditions as myopia, astigmatism, and hyperopia.

The person with normal vision can read the "20 foot row" at a distance of 20 feet. Thus, 20/70 means that the person sees at 20 feet what the individual with normal vision could see at 70 feet.

Snellen's notation and percentage of visual efficiency follows:

20/20	100.00 percent
20/35	87.5 percent
20/70	64.0 percent
20/100	48.9 percent
20/200	20.0 percent

When the school wishes to introduce equipment in order to include more than the Snellen testing, the St. Louis research showed that the Massachusetts Vision Test is very reliable (Foote, 1954). The Massachusetts Vision Test consists of a battery of three tests: (1) tests for distance visual acuity with an illuminated Snellen E Chart, (2) a plus-lens test for hyperopia, and (3) a test for vertical and horizontal muscle imbalances at 20 feet and for near horizontal-muscle imbalance at reading distance. In addition to the Snellen, which is the easiest to administer, and the Massachusetts, the Telebinocular, and Ortho-Rater are most suitable for use in the school.

It should be emphasized here that vision screening programs in schools only indicate the probability and not the proof of possible vision problems. Screening is not to be considered diagnostic. There are many vision tests available for school screening programs. The school will have to decide which test will be most beneficial to their specific population.

The screening tests should be supplemented by careful daily observation by the parents and classroom teachers. The following questions are recommended as a guide for daily observations.

1. Does the child play easily with others in games requiring distance or near vision?

2. Does he progress normally in reading, writing, and drawing activities?

3. Does he complain often of headache, nausea, or dizziness?

4. Is he sensitive to light?

5. Are his eyes often watery or red?

6. Does he have coordination problems in directing gaze of both eyes?

7. Does he rub eyes frequently?

8. Does he often attempt to brush away a blur?

9. Does close work cause the child to cry or become irritable?

10. When looking at distant objects does he screw up face or squint eyes?

Observations by parents and teachers can help to locate children with uncorrected visual defects. Children with suspected eye problems should be recommended for an examination by a specialist in eye problems and corrective measures. This will aid the child in progressing to his ultimate capacity—mentally, socially, and emotionally.

Special attention should be given to the terms *oculist, opthalmologist, optometrist,* and *optician* since there are important distinctions between the types of services which these specialists are qualified to give. The terms *oculist* and *opthalmologist* are used interchangeably, since both titles refer to medical doctors who have specialized in eye problems. The *optometrist* is a person who has specialized in eye problems but does not possess a medical degree, and the *optician* is a craftsman whose job is to grind lenses. Three of the specialists mentioned may write prescriptions for glasses; the prescriptions are to be filled by the optician.

A person should have a full understanding of the qualifications of each type of eye specialist before recommending a child for the services of a particular specialist.

CAUSES

A large number of the partially sighted are affected by prenatal conditions, some of which are hereditary. Other causes may be diseases, accidents, or developmental anomalies. (See Table 4-I.)

TABLE 4-I

CAUSES OF BLINDNESS

Heredity	15%
Infectious diseases	7%
Prenatal causes	50%
Injuries	3%
Poisoning	20%
Tumors	5%
	100%

The following are descriptions of the common refractive errors of vision in children which account for about 50 percent of defective vision:

1. *Myopia,* or nearsightedness, is a lengthening of the diameter of the eyeball from front to back in relation to its focusing power. The object seen is focused ahead of the retina (Fig. 4-1). It is usually corrected by a concave lens (Fig. 4-2).

2. *Hyperopia,* or farsightedness, is a shortening of the eyeball from front to back so that the rays of light focus behind the retina (Fig. 4-3). This condition is corrected by using a convex lens to "bend" the light rays so they will focus on the retina (Fig. 4-4).

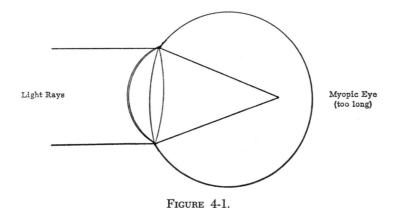

Light Rays

Myopic Eye
(too long)

FIGURE 4-1.

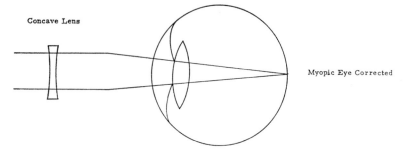

FIGURE 4-2.

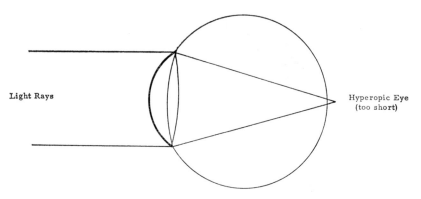

FIGURE 4-3.

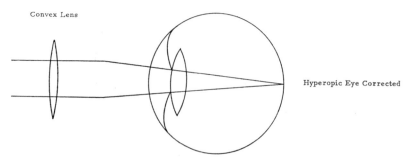

FIGURE 4-4.

3. *Astigmatism* is an irregular curvature of the cornea or of the lens. This prevents rays of light from coming to a single point of focus on the retina. Special glasses usually neutralize this refractive error, but sometimes it is impossible to obtain full correction (Fig. 4-5).

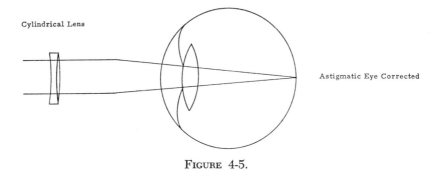

Cylindrical Lens

Astigmatic Eye Corrected

FIGURE 4-5.

Myopes may become introverted, selfish, self-centered, and poorly adjusted socially. Their distance vision is poor, so they usually do not care for sports or competitive games. They resort to reading and close eye work, assuming they are average or above in intelligence.

Hyperopes may become lazy, inattentive, mischievous, and extroverted. They cannot see well for eye work, and may lose interest in reading, writing, arithmetic, and other studies requiring reading.

The following is a list of common developmental anomalies of structure which may cause vision problems:

1. *Cataract* is any opacity of the lens or of its capsule. Surgery is the best method for improving vision in an eye with a cataract, but in some cases the eye is needled and the opacity is broken up and absorbed.

2. *Dislocation of lens* is caused by some defect in the suspensory ligament of the lens. It may be congenital (usually hereditary) or acquired. If acquired, it could be caused by blows to the eye, or by disease degenerating ligaments of the lens. Suitable glasses should be provided for partial dislocation; re-

moval of the lens is necessary if the dislocation is complete.

3. *Albinism* is an inherited condition involving a deficiency of pigment in the iris. This causes the pupils of the eyes to appear pinkish in color. There is defective vision with photophobia (intolerance to light) and nystagmus (rapid involuntary movements of the eyeballs). Treatment consists of tinted, dark, or slit-opening glasses.

4. *Retinitis pigmentosa* is a chronic, progressive, degenerative disease of the retina. It may occur early in childhood or at a later age. The first symptom is night blindness. The visual field is gradually reduced and eventually may be destroyed entirely. There is no known cure or procedure to correct the disease or to stop its progress.

5. *Strabismus,* or crossed eyes, is caused by a weakness of one or more eye muscles; therefore the two eyes do not focus on the same object simultaneously.

The following is a list of common eye diseases which may cause vision problems:

1. *Glaucoma* is a preventable eye disease caused by increased pressure within the eye which causes hardening of the eyeball. The cause is unknown, but the condition does follow a hereditary pattern. When treated early the disease can be controlled and the remaining vision saved.

2. *Ptosis* is the drooping of the upper lid due to deficient development or paralysis of the levator muscles. Usually an operation is needed for correction; sometimes a mechanical device is used to hold up the lid.

3. *Retrolental fibroplasia* is a condition characterized by a detached retina and so named by a Boston opthalmologist, Dr. T. L. Terry, in 1942. Prematurity predisposes this condition. The length of time a premature infant is kept in an oxygen-enriched environment has been proved to be the important factor in the cause of retrolental fibroplasia. This disease was nonexistent before 1938, and by 1955 had almost completely disappeared.

How We See

The sense of vision is indeed complex. An intricate physiological system is involved in good vision. The system must be intact and difficulty in any part may lead to visual handicaps.

The physiological system is surrounded by protective structures. Included among these are the bony eyesockets of the skull, the eyelids, eyelashes, and eyebrows. Another method of protection is provided by the tear system which cleans and lubricates.

The cornea, aqueous humor, lens, and vitreous humor are the vital parts which provide the refraction of light and focus this light on the retina. If an interference interrupts the proper transmission, refraction, and focusing of light, there results faulty vision or blindness. (See Figs. 4-6 and 4-7.)

There are muscles which coordinate and balance the movement of the eyes. Naturally, for proper vision, these muscles have to operate adequately.

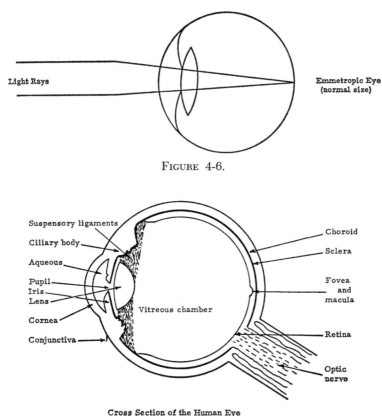

Light Rays

Emmetropic Eye
(normal size)

FIGURE 4-6.

Suspensory ligaments
Ciliary body
Aqueous
Pupil
Iris
Lens
Cornea
Conjunctiva

Vitreous chamber

Choroid
Sclera
Fovea
and
macula
Retina
Optic
nerve

Cross Section of the Human Eye

FIGURE 4-7.

Vision actually takes place in the brain. The retina and optic nerve are part of the brain. Rods and cones—receptor cells —found in the retina are responsible for detail and color vision.

The lens focuses light on the retina. When the point of focus falls behind the retina we call the condition hyperopia or far-sightedness. When the lens focuses the point of light in front of the retina the condition is called myopia or nearsightedness. The convex lens is required to correct farsightedness and the concave lens for nearsightedness. The condition called astigmatism occurs when the cornea is deformed. This blurred vision, resulting from the faulty transmission and refraction of light, is corrected by a cylindrical lens.

German measles, mumps, chickenpox, and many other viral diseases contracted by the mother during the first three months of pregnancy may produce cataracts, pigmentation of the retina, corneal opacities, and microphthalmia (abnormally small eyes).

Kerby, in a national survey of the visual defects found in six hundred classes for partially seeing children which was made by the National Society for the Prevention of Blindness, reports the following findings concerning types and percentage of defective vision (Kerby, 1952):

Refractive errors	49 percent
(myopia, hyperopia, etc.)	
Developmental anomalies of structure	22 percent
(cataracts, albinism, etc.)	
Defects of muscle function	17 percent
(strabismus, nystagmus, etc.)	
Disease or defects of the eye	11 percent
(due to infection, injuries, etc.)	
Others, causes undetermined	1 percent

In a study of 131 partially seeing children (see Table 4-II), Bateman (1963) found a frequency and percentage of eye conditions which corresponds well with Kerby's findings.

THE BLIND

As stated previously in this chapter, many legally blind children can be educated in the regular classroom. For this reason, part of this chapter will be devoted to the blind. Readers should

TABLE 4-II

FREQUENCY AND PERCENTAGE OF EYE CONDITIONS

Condition	Number of Cases	Percent %
Albinism (including albinism with nystagmus)	7	5
Cataracts (including bilateral, unilateral, congential and aphakia)	20	15
Myopia (including progressive, degenerative, myopic astigmatism)	32	24
Myopia with strabismus, esotropia, or nystagmus	7	5
Hyperopia (including hyperopic astigmatism, and with strabismus, nystagmus, or esotropia)	10	8
Retrolental fibroplasis	17	13
Esotropia (including esotropia with nystagmus, and including amblyopia ex anopsia)	11	9
Nystagmus	10	8
Other (optic atrophy, glaucoma, chorioretinitis, etc.)	17	13
Total	131	100

keep in mind that the author is not discussing the totally blind child, but more specifically the child whose vision is close to the yardstick of 20/200 in the best eye after correction.

Definition

The legally blind have a visual acuity of 20/200 or less in the better eye after correction. It is possible for children who are legally blind to read large print and even function as partially sighted. Most of the blind persons in this country are in the 65-and-older age group. The total number of blind persons in the United States is estimated to be about 400,000.

Unspecified prenatal causes account for approximately 50 percent of all blindness. Other causes include infectious diseases, accidents, poisoning, heredity, and tumors.

Characteristics

Myers (1930) found that, out of 2,860 blind children, 50.2 percent were boys and 49.8 percent were girls. As has already been mentioned in this chapter, mental retardation is not a necessary concomitant of blindness. Many studies are available which indicate that partially seeing children do not deviate to any great extent from seeing children as far as intelligence is concerned.

There is much controversy concerning the emotional adjustment of the blind and the partially seeing. Meyerson (1953) has pointed out the many discrepencies in the research concerning the adjustment of this group. Cowen (1961), in one of the most sophisticated studies, found no great difference between the blind in residential schools, the blind in day schools, and a group of seeing students in comparable situations.

Dreams

The dreams of blind children are frequently discussed and many observations have been made but little investigative research into the dreams of these children is available. Deutsch (1928) based her conclusions on her own dreams and indicated that taste and smell played no part in her dreams while hearing played the most important part. She dreamed of having long conversations and actually heard what was being said to her by voices having all their usual inflections. Costa (1937) analyzed the dreams of fifteen children and concluded that the dreams of totally blind chlidren are predominately of an olfactory and auditory nature.

The congenitally blind and those who become blind before the age of five do not have visual dreams. In persons blinded later in life, visual imagery is present in their dreams but it deteriorates in proportion to the duration of the blindness. In a study by Blank (1958) it is pointed out that blind people's dreams also include smell, taste, and temperature perceptions.

Intelligence

Samuel P. Hayes did the 1937 revision of the Stanford-Binet test for the blind, which was named the Interim-Hayes Binet. It was found by Hayes that the mean IQ of the blind is about 99, with fewer blind falling into the superior and normal range when compared with seeing children.

Kirk (1963, p. 202) says, "The available evidence indicates that the development of partially sighted children does not deviate from that of seeing children nor does it show discrepancies in growth within the child." Bateman's (1962) evidence indicated a mean IQ of 100 for 131 children studied.

Education

The education of the blind and partially sighted, as with all persons, begins at birth and continues throughout life. The visually handicapped person has special educational needs which the sighted person does not. These needs are met in varying ways. How these needs are fulfilled and how well they are fulfilled depends upon the degree of disability, the facilities available to the person, and upon the person himself.

The visually handicapped child begins life with the basic needs of any child. Jones (1963) states:

> The child who is handicapped by a visual loss or impairment must have the love and care of his parents just like his normally seeing brothers and sisters. He may have even greater need for their affection if he is to make a healthy adjustment to his defect (p. 6).

Given a comfortable environment, a child whose only handicap is a visual one should acquire many skills at about the same age as a fully sighted child. He should learn to walk, talk, develop independent eating habits, and be toilet trained at about the same age his sighted counterpart would be.

A blind or partially sighted child who is otherwise normal can be taught in preschool and early school years to begin to acquire educational aids such as nonvisual cues. Whitstock suggests the following nonvisual cues:

> A bakery with its characteristic odor which serves to locate it as a landmark, or informs the blind person of its purpose. A trolley has a sound all its own. This sound identified the street as a major thoroughfare, or points out the location of a possible means of transportation. The wind can give a great deal of information: it rustles through the leaves and sighs through pine branches. If constant, it can give a method of checking one's direction. If a person steps past the protection of a building, its unchecked gust identifies an open space adjacent to him. A driveway can act as a landmark and can be distinguished as a break in the sidewalk, or a gravel strip through concrete (pp. 9-10).

These and similar aids can greatly increase a blind child's orientation and mobility.

If possible, a blind or partially seeing child should have nursery school experience with seeing children. Pauline Moore, in her study (1952), found that the teacher of seeing children usually required some reassurance before accepting a blind or partially sighted child as part of her group. The teacher usually had fears concerning the child's safety, the adequacy of the size of the staff, and concern for the common good of the group. Certain standards of readiness were adopted and most of the children in this study met them between three and one-half and five years of age. These standards were not too different from those set for seeing children. However, the children with visual disabilities were usually placed in a group of younger children. Moore concluded that the experiences of the children she followed were most worthwhile: "The independence stressed in a nursery school program was extremely important to all the blind children in helping them to develop initiative and to build confidence in themselves." She also found some carry-over of learning from school to home and the development of many positive attitudes for all the children.

The blind and partially sighted school-age child can be educated in several ways. He can live in a residential school for the blind and partially sighted. He can attend a regular class with seeing children and have a resource room available to him in which he has special materials and aids. He can attend a special class in a regular school or he may be helped by an itinerant teacher. Norris did an interim follow-up study of children whose preschool development had been studied by the multi-disciplinary research team at the University of Chicago. These children were followed through some of their early school years and evaluated for social adjustment and general level of functioning. Some of the children were in day classes in the local school systems, some were in special classes or using resource rooms, and others were in residential schools.

One most important fact was noted in this study. Even though children have problems, they should still have regular eye examinations. Norris (1966) states:

Two of the children in this particular study were transferred from braille programs to programs for the partially sighted after thorough study of their residual vision resulted in the successful fitting of special glasses. Such cases illustrate dramatically the need for continued study of visually handicapped children and the importance of having a variety of school programs available to them, with the selection of a given program determined by the needs of the individual child and his family (p. 23).

Norris concluded:

Given favorable opportunities the blind child can achieve a level of functioning much higher than that usually expected of him and one which compares favorably with that of other children of his chronological age level (p. 23).

Blind and partially sighted children require a variety of special instructional materials. Wherever their education is undertaken, the blind child needs Braille facilities (stylus, slate, Braillewriter) and instruction in their use. He must be taught to read and write with some degree of ease using these facilities. He should have available recorded materials to help him utilize to the fullest his other senses.

The partially sighted child needs books that are suitable for him. In most cases the print must be large. Eakin and his colleagues (1964) found that "time and fatigue are related factors which are extremely significant when measuring the ability to see" (p. 2). They concluded that 18-point type is easiest for the partially seeing child to use (see Fig. 4-8).

As the blind and partially seeing person progresses through school, he must come to have a realistic concept of his abilities and limitations. Some blind persons tend to become over-achievers, particularly those who are pushed by well-meaning people. These persons may perform well academically in high school and desire to go on to do college work. Many blind and partially sighted persons have the ability to profit from more formal education and should be encouraged to go to college. Bauman and Yoder (1962) reported a survey of blind and visually handicapped persons who were successful in professional occupations and told how they had prepared for their college work by using Braillewriters, readers, and friends who made carbons of their notes. They found several workable solutions

LARGE PRINT

Children with some re-
sidual vision are some-
times able to do a part of
their work with their eyes.
This is a sample of the 18
point type which is available on all grade levels for
this purpose. The large
print textbooks parallel
the Braille texts in each
instance.

FIGURE 4-8.

to the problem of taking examinations and generally met and
solved problems of formal education for the blind and partially
sighted.

Many academically successful blind children have difficulty
in gaining admission to the college of their choice or in being
allowed to take specific courses they want after they are
admitted. Some blind are diverted into fields other than the
one of their original choice. In college, however, most receive
advice or counseling as to what courses they can or should take.
As more blind and partially sighted persons receive undergraduate and graduate degrees more colleges will provide opportunities for these people.

Educational Provisions for the Blind

The four most recognized and widely acceptable types of educational provisions for blind children are as follows:

1. Public or private residential schools.

2. Education in public or private schools with the sighted with a resource teacher available all day.

3. Education in public or private schools with the sighted with intinerant teaching at needed periods.

4. Special class placement in public or private schools.

A publication by the U. S. Office of Education (Jones and Collins, 1966, p. 6) states that five basic types of organizational pattern have evolved for visually handicapped children. These patterns are defined as follows:

1. *Full-time special class*—a specially staffed and equipped room in which blind and/or partially seeing children receive three fourths or more of their formal instruction.

2. *Cooperative special class*—a specially staffed and equipped room in which blind and/or partially seeing children are enrolled or registered with the special teacher, but receive less than three fourths of their formal instruction there. The remainder of their school day is in regular classrooms.

3. *Resource room*—a specially staffed and equipped room to which blind and/or partially seeing children who are enrolled or registered in regular classrooms come at scheduled intervals or as the need arises.

4. *Itinerant teacher*—an organizational pattern whereby blind and/or partially seeing children spend most of their school day in regular classrooms but receive special instruction individually or in small groups from itinerant teachers who travel among two or more schools devoting more than half of their time to the instruction of such children.

5. *Teacher consultant*—an organizational pattern whereby special teachers serve as itinerant teachers part of the time but spend 50 percent or more of their time in more general duties, such as consulting with regular school personnel and distributing aids.

Number of Programs

The basic patterns are arranged below in the rank order of frequency of their use during the 1962-63 school year by 353 local school programs (Jones and Collins, 1966, p. 7):

Type of Pattern	Number of Programs Reporting Use
I. Itinerant teacher pattern	140
II. Resource room pattern	137
III. Full-time special class pattern	98
IV. Cooperative special class pattern	72
V. Teacher consultant pattern	37

Slightly more of the 353 programs reported the use of the itinerant teacher pattern than the use of the resource room pattern, but, as can be seen, the number of resource room teachers employed in local school programs exceeded that of teachers in any other type of pattern. A rank order listing of the 1,163 full-time special teachers of visually handicapped children in these programs follows (Jones and Collins, 1966, p. 7):

Type of Teacher	Number
Resource room teachers	428
Itinerant teachers	256
Full-time special class teachers	242
Cooperative special class teachers	183
Teacher consultants	54

Braille

Braille was originally developed by Louis Braille, a Frenchman, in 1829. Braille is a system of "tactile" reading in which the blind person usually reads with one hand and keeps his place vertically with the other (see Fig. 4-9). Grade One Braille is written in full spelling; Grade Two Braille makes use of contractions representing letter combinations, syllables, and words.

There are various devices for writing Braille but the fastest method is the Braille typewriter. Braille can also be written by

BRAILLE ALPHABET AND NUMBERS
USED BY THE BLIND

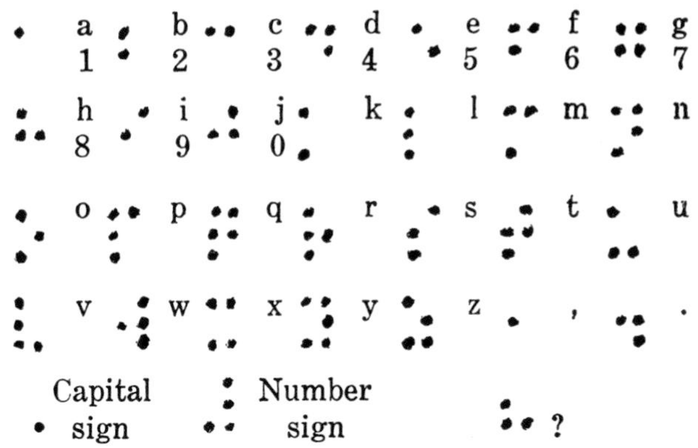

a b c d e f g
1 2 3 4 5 6 7

h i j k l m n
8 9 0

o p q r s t u

v w x y z , ?

Capital sign   Number sign   ?

The Braille System is comprised of signs formed by the use of all the possible combinations of 6 dots numbered and arranged thus: 1 4
2 5
3 6

Letters are capitalized by prefixing dot 6. The first ten letters preceded by the number sign represent numbers. Punctuation marks are formed in the lower part of the cell.

In addition to ordinary print the Braille System provides for the writing of foreign languages, musical scores, mathematical and chemical notations, and other technical matter.

FIGURE 4-9.

hand, using the slate and stylus. The slate is a double metal strip with the lower part marked with cell dots and the upper pitted with corresponding holes. The paper is inserted between the metal strips and with the stylus, a darning-needle-type instrument, dots are embossed through the holes. This has to be read from the opposite side of the paper; therefore the work must be done in reverse, beginning at the right margin and working to the left.

Many systems of Braille have been attempted, but since 1950 Standard English Braille has been used consistently. The systems used include Moon's phonic symbols (modified Roman letters), American Braille, English Braille, and New York Point (a cell two dots high and varying in width). Braille has been adapted in many different forms in various languages including Spanish, Korean, Chinese, and others.

Braille presents a storage problem in an adequately equipped library. To combat this, many libraries borrow from the American Foundation for the Blind and the Library of Congress.

Number of Registered Braille Users

During 1969 there were 22,000 legally blind children registered in private and public residential institutions in the United States. One half of the children registered in these institutions were Bralle users. There were 12,000 children registered in public residential schools and 10,000 children registered in private residential schools. Of the children registered in public schools across the country only 25 percent were Braille users.

In the state of Arkansas sixty children are being supported in the public school system by the large print books and other materials supplied to them by the Arkansas School for the Blind and the State Department of Education. Three Braille users in the state of Arkansas are also enrolled in the public school system. These three children, who are legally blind, are doing very well in the public schools because the school personnel have made an overt effort to take care of their needs.

Problems Encountered

One of the major problems encountered by individuals helping the blind and partially sighted in the regular classroom is the acquisition of textbooks in braille. The textbook adoption system throughout the nation is quite varied. Because it is so varied, there is always the possibility that the textbook adopted in a particular state will not be published in braille. The state departments of education can get these books on tape, but this takes time and very often the school system does not know the textbook to be used until school starts. These books can be blown up through various reproduction procedures but this too is very expensive and time-consuming.

Factors Involved

There are many factors involved in educating a blind or partially seeing child in the regular classroom. There is a possibility that 50 percent of these children enrolled in institutions across the country could be educated in public and private schools if the factors were right. If they had a good home life, if the parents were attentive and the school system supportive, if the mobility problem were solved, and if the children could have industrial arts and other subjects that are required, then their needs could be met in a public school system. Very often, however, the factors are not right and the children are not adequately cared for in the school systems around the country.

Myths Versus Truths

Ashcroft (1963) lists common myths associated with visually limited individuals and the truth concerning these myths. These are presented below because any teacher should benefit from reading them:

Myths	*Truths*
Visually limited children are endowed with extrasensory powers or are compensated by nature for their defects. They have exceptional talents for music. They have supersensitive hearing, touch and taste.	The visually limited have no "ESP" and rather than being provided natural compensation are more likely to have additional limitations. Should they be found to have senses that are more keen or special musical talents they result from increased attention to the other senses, to diligent practice and opportunities for learning.
Residual vision is damaged by use. Reading in bed, in dim light or watching television "ruins" eyes.	Residual vision is lost or atrophied by disuse. We learn to see and the more we "look" the more we "see."
Vision problems are punishment for sin.	Vision problems result from disease, hereditary, and accidental causes.
Visually limited children have "facial vision" for obstacle perception.	Hearing and the use of auditory cues are known to be necessary and sufficient to explain obstacle perception.
Glasses will cure eye problems.	Eye glasses only change the characteristics of the visual stimulus. They do not cure pathological conditions.
All visually limited children are mentally retarded or emotionally disturbed.	Mental retardation and emotional or social disturbance are not *necessary* correlates of lack of vision or the presence of vision problems.

In concluding this chapter, the author would like to list some suggestions by Ashcroft (1963) for helping the visually limited child in the regular classroom:

1. Be alert to the behavioral signs and physical symptoms of visual difficulties in all children. Be sure that proper referrals have been made and everything possible has been done to correct or ameliorate the problems.

2. Accept and provide for a wide range of individual differences on many dimensions, including vision.

3. View the visual limitation of the child as only one of his attributes, and not as if it was his most important characteristic. Many children have been "taught" to be handicapped and visual limitations have become the central focus in their lives because they were responded to as if the loss was paramount.

4. Make the visually limited child one of your pupils as much as you would any other. Do not consider him the residential school's, the resource teacher's, or the itinerant teacher's responsibility.

5. Provide a setting for, and expect achievement of, the pupil in terms of his scholastic aptitude and other attributes not in terms of visual disability. Differentiate the effects of limitations in vision from effects that have the source in other causes such as emotions, intellect, hearing, attitudes, background. Do not let the child exploit his visual limitation for special treatment.

6. Provide lesson presentations which appeal to, and utilize other senses as well as, vision. Teachers are usually gratified at the results of such efforts for all their children.

7. Arrange preferential seating for the visually limited child, as you would for the needs of any other child, but especially in terms of his range of vision and his needs for differential illumination.

8. Provide a visual environment conducive to comfortable eye work conditions for all children. A good visual environment is characterized in part by fifty foot candles of light on working surfaces, minimized glare, reduction in work-background contrast and provision of controlled lighting for different work and eye condition needs.

9. Obtain assistance in the form of constructive consultation and specialized materials and equipment from those who assume special responsibilities for visually limited children.

10. Help the child to develop concepts meaningful to him and in line with his own reality. Do not impose upon him artificial concepts he cannot understand or appreciate because of his visual limitations.

11. Develop a genuine respect for the child's media for learning (braille, large type; audio and tangible aids; his specialized tools for

learning). Many of these can also enrich the education of all the children.

12. Remember that the visually limited child, perhaps only somewhat more than all children, needs first-hand experiences in preference to vicarious ones.

13. If the regular classroom teacher and the child have access to services from a resource or itinerant teacher, their roles should be clearly delineated. Do not expect the special teacher to re-teach what is supposed to have been taught in the regular classroom. The special teacher's role is to facilitate learning (more than to teach directly) through assistance to the regular teacher and to the child. Do not let the child "pit" or "play" one teacher "against" the other.

14. It is easy to exploit the visually limited child by showing him off to other children, teachers, or to visitors. Treat him as you would any other pupil.

15. When in doubt, the regular teacher should do what she would consider best for any child.

16. Respect for and acceptance of individual differences are learned. These take time and effort. The regular classroom teacher should "give them a try."

REFERENCES

Ashcroft, Samuel C.: Blind and partially seeing children. In Dunn, Lloyd M.: *Exceptional Children in the Schools.* New York, Holt, Rinehart and Winston, 1963.

Bateman, Barbara Dee. Reading and Psycholinguistic Processes of Partially Seeing Children. Unpublished doctoral dissertation, University of Illinois, 1962.

Bateman, Barbara D.: Reading and psycholinguistic processes of partially seeing children. *CEC Research Monograph, No. 5.* Washington, The Council for Exceptional Children, 1963.

Bauman, Mark K., and Yoder, Norman M.: *Placing the Blind and Visually Handicapped in Professional Occupations.* U. S. Department of Health, Education, and Welfare, 1962.

Blank, H. R.: Dreams of the blind. *Psychoanalytic Quarterly, 27,* 1937.

Costa, A.: Sogni difanciulli ciechie semiveggenti. *Rivista de Psicologica, 33,* 1937.

Cowen, E. L., *et al.*: *Adjustment to Visual Disability in Adolescence.* New York, American Foundation of the Blind, 1961.

Deutsch, Elinor: The dream imagery of the blind. *Psychoanalytic Review, 5,* 1928.

Eakin, Pratt, McFarland: *Type Size Research for Partially Seeing Child Project.* Pittsburgh, Stanwix House, 1964.

Fink, W. H.: Ocular defects in preschool children. *The Sight Saving Review*, 1954.

Foote, Franklin M., and Crane, Marian M.: An evaluation of vision screening. *Exceptional Children, 20*, 1954.

Hathaway, Winifred: *Education and Health of the Partially Seeing Child*, 4th ed. New York, Columbia University Press, 1959.

Jones, John Walker: *The Visually Handicapped Child*. U. S. Department of Health, Education, and Welfare, Bulletin 39, 1963.

Jones, John Walker, and Collins, Anne P.: *Educational Programs for Visually Handicapped Children*. U. S. Government Printing Office, Bulletin 6, 1966.

Kerby, Edith C.: A report on visual handicaps of partially seeing children. *Journal of Exceptional Children, 18*, 1952.

Meyers, Edward T.: A survey of sight-saving classes in the public schools of the United States. *The Sight-Saving Class Exchange*. New York, National Society for the Prevention of Blindness, 1930.

Meyerson, L.: The visually handicapped. *Review of Educational Research, 23*, 1953.

Moore, Pauline M.: *A Blind Child, Too, Can Go To Nursery School*. American Foundation for the Blind, Pre-school Series No. 1, 1952.

Norris, Miriam: *The School Age Blind Child Project*. American Foundation for the Blind, 1966.

Whitstock, Robert H.: *Orientation and Mobility for Blind Children*, Commission for the Blind, New York State Booklet No. 204.

Chapter 5

THE SPEECH-HANDICAPPED IN THE REGULAR CLASSROOM

SPEECH OR ORAL communication is the primary tool by which an individual relates to others in the world around him. Speech involves more than the ability to make sounds or to pronounce words. It calls for the assimilation of sounds into words, followed by a combination of words into units which make a meaningful whole. Therefore, speech becomes the basic tool which assists in developing a formalized language. It is the result of visual, auditory, kinesthetic, and perceptual experiences and has as its aim the conveyance of an assembly of ideas to a listener.

The child having a speech handicap has always functioned adequately in the regular classroom, assuming of course he does not have other handicaps. Specialists should be available to help the speech-handicapped child in the regular and special classrooms and also to help the teachers to work with mild speech problems.

Since the early history of man society has been concerned with human communication. All societies use vocalizations in communicating, even though some societies do not have a written form of language.

The concern for individuals having defective speech predates man's concern for normal speech. As early as 340 B.C. man was trying to find a "cure" for stuttering. This concern which began hundreds of years ago has reached down through the ages to our present time.

Speech and the need to express ourselves adequately is of paramount importance in this most vocal of worlds. An agile tongue is to be envied. Oral speech forms the very core of our communication with our peers. It is something upon which we rely practically every day of our lives. The ordinary business of life presents many opportunities for the use of oral communication. And not only is it a transmissive thing; psychologists have shown that the ability to "think aloud" has become an economic necessity. We win and lose jobs, not on how little or how much we know, but rather on how well we are able to "sell" ourselves and our talents.

Obviously, then, there is a large responsibility on us as parents, teachers, and specialists in the field of speech to see that every child has the opportunity to develop his speech skills to the fullest—a facility which our society so highly rewards both in school and in later life. And since these skills are a product of the learning process, it is only natural that many will fall by the wayside as the result of some hindrance. These latter ones will be the focal point of our discussion.

Since this chapter concerns correcting speech defects, it is deemed necessary to preface all remarks with a few facts and statistics concerning disorders of speech.

RECOGNIZING SPEECH DISORDERS

In order to correct speech defects one must be able to recognize speech disorders. Let us consider, "What is a speech defect?" According to Van Riper (1963), speech is defective "when it deviates so far from the speech of other people that it calls attention to itself, interfers with communication, or causes its possessor to be maladjusted." Or, condensing this somewhat, we might say that speech is defective when it is conspicuous, unintelligible, or unpleasant.

Berry and Eisenson (1956), in their definition, include an additional subjective aspect. They propose that speech may be considered defective when the speaker becomes excessively self-conscious or apprehensive about objectively small deviations; or assumed deviation, however small, becomes a significant defect if it interferes with the speaker's social adjustment. We could sum it up in one sentence. Speech is defective when it deviates. But who is to judge? The cultural norms of society really determine how deviant speech must be before it is conspicuous. For example, we would not consider a child of three who said "wabbit" for "rabbit" as having a speech defect, whereas it would be uncommon among adults. Defective speech is characterized in the following descriptions (Berry and Eisenson, 1956):

1. It is not easily audible.
2. It is not readily intelligible.
3. It is vocally unpleasant.
4. It deviates in respect to specific sound (consonants, vowel, or diphthong) production.
5. It is labored in production.
6. It is linguistically deficient.
7. It is inappropriate to the speaker in terms of age, sex, and physical development.
8. It is visibly unpleasant.

TYPES OF SPEECH DISORDERS

As one can easily see, it is apparent that much can be wrong with the manner in which an individual speaks. In fact the range of defects is so wide, Van Riper (1963) has conveniently divided them into four categories: articulation, time (or rhythm), voice, and symbolization (language). It would help the reader understand corrective techniques better if we review briefly speech disorders in general. For this we will select one classification and describe corrective measures. It is far beyond the scope of this chapter to discuss them all.

Articulation

Under disorders of articulation we include all those disorders characterized by the substitution, omission, addition, and distortion of the speech sounds. A child who omits the "s" might say, "In the 'ummer, I like to 'wim, 'kate, and ride my bi'ycle." One who makes additions would say, "My umburella is bluack and grueen." There are several concomitant terms related to these disorders, namely, baby talk, sometimes called infantile perseveration and characterized by sound substitutions during the early stages of child development; lalling, which is due to sluggishness of the tongue tip and characterized by defective "a, l, t, d, or s" sounds; lisping, a disorder of the "s" and "z" sounds and a frequent one; delayed speech, unintelligible consonants; and oral inaccuracy, a general term for any mild articulatory defect. One must keep in mind that these defects do not always occur independently but may appear jointly in an individual's speech. For example, a laller may also lisp or a lisper may talk baby talk.

Many people would tend to overlook articulatory defects as being serious. Some even think that it is cute in children. Although most children outgrow their speech difficulties, there are many who do not. Of the 5 percent of children having serious speech defects, 3 percent of the total have problems of articulation (ASHA Committee on the Midcentury White House Conference, 1952). One estimate states that there are approximately 120,000 children of school age that have functional articulatory defects (Berry and Eisenson, 1956). This figure justifies therapy. In working with speech defectives, the number of articulatory errors is sometimes so great that the speech is nothing more than an unintelligible jargon (idioglessia). Corrective procedures for articulatory errors will be discussed later.

Time and Rhythm

The second major category of disorders is that of time and rhythm. We speak language in a sequential pattern in that sound follows sound, syllable follows syllable. When something disrupts the spontaneous flow of speech to the degree that it is conspicuous, unpleasant, or unintelligible, we have a disorder of time. A prime example is the stutterer. A disorder which has affected men through the ages, it ranks second, after articulatory disorders. About 280,000 school-age children are gripped by this perplexing problem. An interesting thing about stuttering is that it seems to be more of a communicative disorder than one of speech. Most stutterers speak fluently when alone or singing. The impediment appears while under emotional stress or while confronted with others in a speaking situation. There have been many books written on the subject and presently several theories are being considered as to the cause or causes. Johnson (1956), an authority in the field, claims that stuttering is a symptom of psychoneurosis or due to some physical difference. Early recognition and referral of a stutterer to a trained therapist is an excellent recommendation for it may save much anxiety, frustration, and embarrassment in later years.

Cluttering is also a disorder of time or rhythm. Distinguished from stuttering, it is characterized by excessive speed in speaking, disorganized sentence structure, and slurred or omitted syllables and sounds.

Voice

The third category of speech defects is that of voice disorders (dysphonia). As mentioned previously, the sounds of speech may be articulated incorrectly, and the noises, sounds, and tones themselves may be defective. If so, we have a voice problem. Estimates indicate that less than 0.5 percent to more than 1 percent may have difficulties in vocalization (ASHA Committee on the Midcentury White House Conference, 1952, and Johnson, Brown, Curtis, Edney, and Keaster, 1956). Some of the possibilities for voice disorders are too-high pitch, too-low pitch, monotone, pitch breaks, and stereotyped inflections (Van Riper, 1963). There may be disorders in voice intensity or loudness and voice quality. Examples might be voices that are too weak or too loud, hypernasal, strident, falsetto, breathy, or hoarse.

Symbolization

The fourth category of disorders concerns problems of symbolic formulation and expression (dysphasia.) Speech and all the language functions may be affected singly or jointly because of brain damage. Although these individuals comprise a small percentage of speech defectives, they are no less important. Aphasia is a handicap that is often difficult to diagnose. The aphasic may suffer from one or two types: (1) inability to express ideas through spoken or written language symbols (expressive) and (2) disturbance in the ability to comprehend language through spoken or written symbols (receptive) (Wepman, 1951). Therapy for aphasics presents many frustrations and challenges for the speech therapist.

Related Speech Disorders

Mention must be made of other related speech disorders. There are those of cleft palate, foreign accent, deaf and hard-of-hearing speech, and cerebral palsy. These disorders do not always appear as distinctive entities. One might have a combination of several defects. Although these latter ones mentioned comprise relatively small numbers, they, along with stuttering, present great difficulties in treatment.

CORRECTION

With this potpourri of information it is evident that speech pathology is no simple matter. Volumes could be written on corrective techniques and methods for the above disorders. Time does not allow a comprehensive analysis of corrective measures for each disorder; however, this brief look at speech disorders in general provides us a better understanding of the many types of defects and the difficulties that have befallen the speech clinician. Remarks will be restricted primarily to methods used in correction of articulatory errors, the ones most commonly found and a favorite of clinicians.

Diagnosis and Evaluation

The two most commonly used terms referring to the presumed etiology or causation of articulatory errors are dyslalia and dysarthria. The first refers to disorders of functional origin where the cause may be due to mislearning, imitation, emotional conflicts, or the like. Dysarthria implies a disorder of articulation due to impairment of the part of the central nervous system which directly controls the muscles of articulation.

Defects of articulation comprise the bulk of speech disorders. Hundreds of surveys prove this. Much to the clinicians' delight, articulatory cases respond most easily and quickly to therapy, but there are many exceptions to this rule.

Most parents want to begin immediately to correct a child

who says "whittle" for "little." They feel the child has made a mistake and should correct it. The speech clinician takes a different approach. He must come to grips with the problem. Like the detective or lawyer, he must get to the "facts." He attempts to answer the questions: "Why does the child have articulatory errors?" "What are the errors?" and finally, "What must be done to eliminate them?"

One of the first duties of the clinician in any thorough analysis is to consider the developmental factors. This is on the assumption that the child has been referred. He should explore the maturation of articulation in the child. This would come from parent interviews. All of the child's past history should be investigated to determine the origin of the problem. Any illness, accident, or abnormalities in growth could be significant. The child's hearing acuity and intelligence quotient need to be known. Also it is helpful to know the amount of speech stimulation in the home and the attitude of the parents toward the defect. Often the cause is lost somewhere in the midst of speech development. An earlier cause that was highly effective in contributing to the defect may have since subsided while the defect persists. Then, too, there is the possibility of speech being mislearned. A child may habitually say "thoup" because of poor teaching. And we must not forget emotional factors, often important in cases of delayed speech. This preliminary investigation and history taking is basic. Misdiagnosis is a curse to any true speech clinician.

Some parents believe that their child has faulty articulation due to organic abnormalities. Misarranged teeth, swollen tonsils, and a shortened frenum (tongue-tie) are often suspected. However, speech clinicians are usually conservative in attributing the defective sounds to organic factors (Van Riper, 1963). There are on record too many instances of good, intelligible speech when organic factors are present. There are those who have no teeth who produce all the speech sounds correctly. There are individuals with no tongue or with half of their tongue who speak intelligibly. It is possible to compensate. A perfectly good "l" sound may be produced with the tongue-tip down or even outside the mouth. The difference lies in the extra effort in learning to overcome these obstacles. This does not mean that the clinician should discount organic deviations entirely, but he should consider them along with the many other possible causes.

Modern surgery has done wonders in the reconstruction of dental, palatal, and jaw structures. Although most undertakings of this sort are tremendously expensive, it is the duty of the clinician to refer those with marked mouth deformities to these specialists. Especially in cases of severe organic defects in children, the speech clinician should convince the parents of the need for corrective measures. One way is to point out the social maladjustment which such defects may produce.

Another important factor in any satisfactory diagnosis is a complete phonetic analysis of the individual's speech. This is vitally important for therapy. Van Riper (1963) gives three major objectives in making a phonetic analysis: "(1) Find the sounds which are defective; (2) the type of error in terms of substitution, omission, insertion, or distortion; and (3) the location of the error within the word (initial, medial, or final)." This gives us an idea of which sound or sounds are defective, and how much ear training is needed. It helps the therapist understand better the scope of the problem. You ask, "What method do you use to find these errors?" Most therapists use a standard picture articulation test. For adults, special phonetically structured sentences are often used. One of the best is the Developmental Picture Articulation Test by Henja. The Bryngleson and Glaspey Picture Articulation Test is also widely used among speech therapists. The pictures are arranged in sequential order of the development of consonant sounds. They begin with the plosives (p, b) and run through the completion of the blends like *sl*ed and um*br*ella. After gaining rapport with the child, he is asked to say aloud the pictures . On a scoring blank, the therapist records phonetically any misarticulated sound, whether it is at the beginning, middle, or end of a word. This is getting the child's errors down on paper so that the clinician can see the problem in better perspective.

It is advantageous for the therapist to carry the evaluation a step further and get a kinetic analysis. It is not just enough to say a child has a lisp. We need to determine whether it is a lateral, occluded, interdental, or nasal formation of the lisp. In short, the important thing is the manner of production. An attempt is made to find just what the child is doing when he makes an error. One method is for the clinician to imitate or duplicate what the child is doing. Each of the speech sounds may be incorrectly produced in several ways. For example, errors of stop-plosives such as "k" and "g" seem to be due to (1) the wrong location of the tongue contact, (2) the wrong speed in forming the contacts, and (3) the wrong structures used in contacts. A child who says "tandy" for "candy" is using a tongue-palatal contact, but it is too far forward. Too slow a release from a "k" contact may give a breathy, aspirate quality to the utterance. "Kuheep the kueys" is an example of this (Van Riper, 1963).

A common error is the use of the wrong channel for the airstream. This is seen when using an unvoiced "l" for the "s." A lateral lisp is produced. Also the airstream may be in the wrong direction as in the case of a nasal lisp. The "s" is inhaled. Too weak an air pressure may cause an omission of sounds.

The reproduction of the error enables the therapists to understand its nature. Only after careful analysis of the articulatory error and breaking of the old habit can the clinician begin any thorough sessions. Most progress can be made after the subject understands clearly what he is doing wrong. Insight into error is a must before significant progress can be made.

A final factor to be considered in an evaluation is the condition under which errors occur. We need to examine each error in terms of the following: (1) type of communicative situation, (2) speed of utterance, (3) kind of communicative material, and (4) discrimination ability (Van Riper, 1963). Some lispers only have difficulty when under emotional stress. Children may imitate correctly but distort their own speech sounds. Knowing when a child makes his errors helps in the therapy.

At the end of the examination all of the information is put together in a systematic and meaningful way. If the therapy plan is to be successful, the information gained must be organized.

The following is a form commonly used:

Case: *Age:*   *Grade:*   *Address:*   *Phone:*

Family history:
Developmental history:
Birth history:
Present physical conditions:
Behavior:
Type of disorder:
Phonetic errors:
Intelligence:
Hearing acuity:
Muscular coordination:
General observation of speech:

The clinician is now ready for therapy. So far this chapter has described defects that would be corrected in individual therapy. For the most part, this will be the major concern of speech clinicians. However, speech therapy can be accomplished by other methods. There are several approaches being used to reach and help those with speech handicaps. One could be referred to as a general speech improvement program.

A General Speech Improvement Program

What is meant by general speech improvement? Ainsworth (1948, p. 46) states, "It is group work done with whole classes or grades. The objectives are to raise the general speech performance of the group and minimize and correct minor defects of some of the individuals in the group."

Van Riper and Butler (1955) propose:

> Speech improvement—is more than tongue exercises, memorization, vocal phonics, articulation, drills, and activities. It is more than instruction in the improvement of voice quality, pitch and intensity. It is more than training in the ebb and flow of speech rhythms. It is more than the sum total of all these parts. Speech improvement should go far beyond the mechanics of speech drills, into the area of meaningful language. One of the most important aims might well be to help the children to verbalize their thought—to be able to "think on their feet" efficiently and adequately (p. 3).

This type of program utilizes group instruction as the basis for speech therapy. Used primarily at the preschool and elementary level, it emphasizes increased vocabulary, growth in concepts, meaning of words, and improved articulation and sentence patterns. The purpose is to develop better communication and language, not just improved articulation or speech production. A program such as this will utilize the classroom teacher and a trained speech pathologist acting as consultant and diagnostician. Only in the regular classroom situation can language development be made to meet the immediate needs of the children.

What is done in the classroom? The therapist may visit the classroom twice a week or more with sessions lasting fifteen to thirty minutes. Each group will receive planned language development programming worked out with the cooperation of the classroom teacher to fit in with the needs, interests, and present academic work of the group. The classroom teacher will remain in the room during the session so that the activities can be repeated at other times and recommendations for future sessions made.

The child is taught common language patterns appropriate in various life situations. Some particular speech patterns might be as follows:

> "Yes." "May I get——?" "Thank you."
> "No." "Have a——." "Hello."
> "Look at——." "Come——."

These patterns are introduced through specific types of activities which encourage the child to take part in conversation and to express ideas or opinions. He needs to learn that speech is a tool which we use for communicative relationships with other people.

Another approach used to reach those with defective speech is the organized speech correction program within the public school system. Ainsworth (1948) divides the work of the speech therapist into two principal categories: correcting speech defects and organizing and administering the speech correction program. From the therapeutic point of view this is similar to individual therapy in that children with pronounced speech defects are the objective rather than general speech improvement. In this program the majority of the work is done in small groups of three and four. Of course this does not rule out individual work. Each case will vary and require certain adjustments.

Individual cases are usually those of a more serious nature such as stuttering, aphasia, or cleft palate. Most speech and hearing clinics provide services for these individuals.

For most people, the field of speech pathology is new. One might ask, "What do speech clinicians do in correcting a defect?" or, "How do they go about it?" To answer these questions and to provide an illustration, let's take a hypothetical case of a child with an articulatory disorder. We will presume that he has been evaluated and found to have defective "s" sounds. Further, we will assume that the child has no significant organic anomaly of the articulatory apparatus. As a rule, children with one error-sound present no major difficulty, but those who have many errors do.

A Hypothetical Case

The first task at hand is to convince the child that he has a problem which he must solve. This is easier said than done. Often speech defectives grow into adulthood without being made aware of their speech disorder. The quickest way of getting rid of an error is to make the child aware of it. After this is accomplished, we hopefully move on. The therapy itself is focused upon the defective sound "s." Parents and teachers often focus their therapy on the word level. "Don't say thitherth," they command. "Say scissors?" This is difficult for the child who has no concept that he is saying it incorrectly. Then, too, suppose he does happen to say it correctly by accident. There is very little carry-over into other words. The speech clinician begins at the sound level (phoneme), then moves to the syllable, word, and sentence level. With this method, once a sound is learned, it is readily incorporated into words containing that sound. The child need not learn each word individually. Although other approaches are used, the majority of speech therapists seem to prefer this method.

Ear Training

In teaching a child to make a sound correctly, clinicians use ear training. The child learns the standard sound through auditory stimulation rather than repetition of syllables or words. The lisper can learn when the sound is distorted and when it is not. To accomplish this the speech therapist uses four basic sets of techniques: (1) isolation (2) stimulation (3) identification and (4) discrimination (Van Riper, 1963).

In isolation, the clinician attempts to break down word configurations so that the correct sound may be heard by itself. To the speech defective, spoken words are lumps of sounds. Sometimes the correct sound is lost somewhere within the word. They do not hear it with clarity. The speech therapist attempts to motivate the child via games and play activities. Two exercises might be as follows: (1) The teacher hides, in different places about the room, nine or ten pictures of various objects, one of which begins with the "s" sound. The moment the child finds this picture, he can run to the teacher's desk and ring a bell. (2) The teacher sounds out words and asks the child to locate the appropriate picture, putting all "s" word pictures in a special envelope.

Second, the child's ear must be bombarded with the sound so thoroughly that it may almost be said to ring in his ears. This is stimulation. The child's attention must be focused to the sound. Parents, friends, and classmates can help. The child makes no attempt on his own to produce the sound. The all important thing is learning to listen. Young children must be motivated to listen by interesting activities. It is a good practice to always let the child perform in some manner to indicate his efficiency in the reception of the stimulation. One activity among many would be the use of a hollow tube of sorts. It is held to the child's ear as he winds a string upon a spool. The clinician makes the sound into the tube. The moment the clinician stops making the sound, the child must stop winding.

In identification, the therapist gives the sound a name. The "s" sound could be called the "snake" or the "leaky-tire" sound. In this way, the sound takes on the identity of sounds with which they work. This helps the child in recognition. Identification is necessary before the final step—discrimination.

The first three steps in ear training must be successful before the therapist begins discrimination. Here, we attempt to compare and contrast the correct and incorrect sounds. It is important that the child be able to differentiate the correct sound from error. Activities are planned so that the child will have to perform to either the correct or incorrect sound by the clinician.

Upon completion of the ear training period, the child should have acquired a clear concept of the target sound. Until now he has not been required to produce the sound. Next comes the transitional step of self-hearing, a process where the child learns to recognize and identify his errors.

Reproducing the Correct Sound

At last comes the big day. The child begins learning to produce the new sound. Keep in mind that the new sound must have been mastered on all the previous levels. There are several ways to approach this task. The speech clinician selects one, often to discard it for another. One has to adapt to each particular case. Learning the new sound is a process of modifying the old sound. Rarely does a child suddenly shift from saying "wabbit" to "rabbit." Change is gradual, for movement of the articulators and acoustical patterns has to be varied.

One method in teaching the new sound is progressive approximation. This method resembles the way that infants acquire normal articulation. The clinician makes the same error as the child. He then makes modifications in the sound and attempts several series of transitional sounds that come closer to the desired or correct sound. This is a gradual process but has been used with great success.

Auditory stimulation is another method. The child attempts to directly imitate the clinician. It works well with those who are ear-minded. Some say the sound perfectly on the first attempt. Others may repeat several times. If the child whispers the sound first, it helps to get the "feel" of it.

The traditional approach is that of phonetic placement. Many elaborate devices and diagrams have been made to show the individual exactly how the sound is to be produced. The disadvantage is that the mechanics of phonetic placement cannot be performed quickly enough for the smooth flow of connected speech. Also many speech clinicians produce sounds in nonstandard ways. If used effectively this method can be an indispensable tool in the kit of the speech clinician. It can give a clear idea of the desired position of the articulators before any speech attempt.

Another useful approach in teaching a new sound is the key-word method. Speech defectives need some standard with which to compare their speech attempts at correct production of the usually defective sound (Van Riper, 1963). Surprisingly, most speech defectives have a few words in which they do not make the error. If the clinician has a keen ear and can capture these words, they will prove to be a tremendous asset. By capitalizing on these key words, he can drill on them, demonstrating that the individual can make the sound correctly in some instances. It is hoped that the defective speaker will be able to produce the new sound in isolation and at will.

Using the Sound in Speech

After our child has learned to make the correct "s" sound, then comes the stabilization. The formation of a new sound is a weak creature and must be reinforced by constant practice. Even then the therapy is not complete. It must now proceed through the syllable, word, and sentence levels. Until now we have been concerned only with the sound itself. As the child progresses from one stage to another, the idea is to make the sound habitual and consistent at all times. It must be unconsciously retained.

One successful method is the use of negative practice. Although it seems odd at first, this is the deliberate and voluntary use of the incorrect sound. Used more with adolescents and adults than children, it is an effective technique for getting the correct sound into an individual's speech. It helps make the sound habitual. The clinician never asks the subject to use the sound incorrectly unless he can produce it correctly whenever called upon. How does it work? (1) It helps make the speech defective conscious of his habit. This is a prerequisite for any elimination of the defect to take place. (2) Voluntary practice makes the error vivid, making the individual vigilant in guarding against it.

It must be remembered that an ideal situation has been discussed, one seldom encountered in therapy. Each individual case is different, requiring constant evaluation. What works in one instance may not be satisfactory in another. Also the proper approach depends upon the type of disorder. There are many variables to be considered.

The possibilities for correction of a speech defect are considerably better than those several centuries ago. We know now that a stutterer is not really a creature possessed by spirits and that society will not be improved by ridiculing and alienating the speech-handicapped. Our enlightenment as to the nature and causes of speech defects and the recognition of them as obstacles to the emotional and social well-being of individuals give promise to those who constantly hide behind a wall of embarrassment.

Speech Therapy as a Profession

It must be stressed that speech therapy as a profession is still very young, with the American Speech and Hearing Association, its professional organization, being established less than fifty years ago. Nevertheless, this profession has branched out internationally. Speech and hearing specialists can be found in most countries throughout the world.

Because of the high standards demanded of the personnel in this field, parents of speech-defective children can feel confident of receiving competent treatment from certified speech or hearing specialists. Also, because of the newness of the field and the high standards enforced, the demand for workers is great. Many college students do not become familiar with the field as a profession until it is too late to start training in this area. However, students who do investigate this field find dedicated professionals working in a still young but rewarding field of service.

Remedial Speech Services

If all children who are of school age in the United States and who have serious speech handicaps were brought together in one place, they would make a city about the size of Philadelphia, which is the nation's fourth largest city. A conservative estimate of the number of these children would be 2,500,000 which exceeds the population of the entire state of Mississippi or Arkansas. As a matter of fact, this figure exceeds the populations of twenty-three of our fifty states. This is a conservative estimate and includes only those children aged five through nineteen who have a speech or hearing defect which is so marked that they go through life with a serious handicap—vocationally, socially, and personally. Speech-handicapped children constitute the largest group of exceptional individuals within our total population and also the largest group who need special education services in the country's elementary and secondary schools. Most of these children are found in the regular classes in the schools of America. It is true that many of them are found in the special classes, too, because the lower the intelligence and the greater the multiple handicaps, the greater the relationship between these abnormalities and speech defects. Nevertheless, most of these children enter the regular first grade classes every year and stay in regular education with the regular class teacher day in and day out. The majority of these handicapped children do not have the services of a speech pathologist. There is no doubt that if these children have average or above intelligence, or even below-average intelligence for many of them, they should be functioning in a regular classroom. There is also no doubt that a speech clinician should be available not only to help the teacher work with speech handicap problems in the regular classroom but also to work with the severely speech-handicapped on a one-to-one basis.

There is an increasing awareness on the part of educators concerning the shortage of speech specialists who are adequately trained to help speech-handicapped children and to help the teacher take care of children with mild defects in the regular classroom or in the special classroom. Today the requirement to meet certification as a speech clinician by the American Speech and Hearing Association is a master's degree. Other individuals who do not hold a master's degree can be certified with a Certificate of Clinical Competence for the members who desire it and can show adequate competence resulting from specialized training and experience. The American Speech and Hearing Association has more than 10,000 members who are actively employed; of these, 7,500 are in clinical work. This is not enough to meet the nation's needs. Therefore the regular classroom teacher should take courses in speech pathology and language development to help him alleviate the mild problems which he will find in his classroom.

An adequate school program requires one trained speech clinician for each 100 speech-handicapped children enrolled in that community. The adults should have two trained speech clinicians for every 50,000 of the total population of a city or community. Therefore one can see that we have a tremendous shortage of speech clinicians in America today. The regular class teacher must in some way help to alleviate the mild speech problems which are found in the classroom. A speech clinician must be available in an adequate program to help the children having severe problems. Regardless of whether the speech clinician is available or whether the regular class teacher is trained to help alleviate these minor problems, we do have children in the regular classes, in special classes, and in other facilities who have mild and severe speech problems. Many of these children receive no service to help alleviate these problems. This is a tragedy and must be alleviated in the very near future if we are going to say that we have adequate programs in all phases of education in the American school system.

We must be reminded that the regular classroom teacher cannot be expected to undertake time-consuming tasks on behalf of pupils who have severe speech impediments. Naturally, a one-to-one relationship would distract the teacher from her main job—that of taking care of the individual differences of all the children in the classroom. The kind of classroom or school system that has a teacher who is good for a child who stutters or has an articulatory disorder is good for all the other children, too.

REFERENCES

Ainsworth, Stanley: *Speech Correction Methods.* New York, Ronald Press, 1951.

ASHA Committee on the Midcentury White House Conference. Speech disorders and speech correction. *Journal of Speech and Hearing Disorders, 17* (No. 2), 1952.

Berry, Mildred R., and Eisenson, Jon: *Speech Disorders.* New York, Appleton-Century-Crofts, 1956.

Johnson, Wendell: *Stuttering in Children and Adults.* Minneapolis, University of Minnesota Press, 1956.

Johnson, Wendell; Brown, S.; Curtis, J.; Edney, C., and Keaster, S.: *Speech Handicapped School Children.* New York, Harper and Brothers, 1956.

Van Riper, Charles: *Speech Correction Principles and Methods.* Englewood Cliffs, N. J., Prentice-Hall, 1963.

Van Riper, Charles, and Butler, K.: *Speech in the Elementary Classroom.* New York, Harper and Brothers, 1955.

Wepman, J. M.: *Recovery From Aphasia.* New York, Ronald Press, 1951.

Chapter 6

THE PARTIALLY HEARING CHILD IN
THE REGULAR CLASSROOM

T HE PARTIALLY HEARING child has always been a member of the regular classroom. Until the development of the pure-tone audiometer and the hearing aid, however, he was usually classified as a troublemaker because of his inability to hear the teacher or the recitation of his classmates.

Wooden (Dunn, 1963) describes the partially hearing as those for whom the loss of hearing is educationally significant, but whose residual hearing is sufficient for interpreting speech with or without the use of a hearing aid. The educationally hard-of-hearing possess hearing levels of 30 to 59 decibels or a little higher.

This chapter deals with the educationally hard-of-hearing and does not refer to the child who is profoundly deaf. The children mentioned in this chapter have a hearing impairment but still possess functional hearing with or without a hearing aid. This chapter, when referring to handling the educational needs of the hearing-impaired in the regular classroom, is not referring to the child who is born deaf or who lost his hearing before acquiring speech and language.

EARLY EDUCATION

The early education of the deaf child is very important. Of the children currently enrolled in schools for the deaf in the United States, 10 percent are under six years of age. The private and residential schools for the deaf also have a large number of preschool children enrolled.

Most deaf children are deaf from birth or before they have

developed speech sufficiently to have obtained a permanent mastery of it. This means that most deaf children are deaf before reaching school age. About two fifths of all deafness is congenital and the remaining is accounted for by diseases and accidents, but more often by diseases. The diseases primarily responsible are meningitis, scarlet fever, measles, whooping cough, and abcesses of the ear and head.

Most parents have a difficult time accepting the fact that they have a deaf child and tend to hope that the child is just slow in developing. But because the infant cannot hear, he becomes handicapped very early; this handicapping process starts at the age of about three months. Naturally infants receive enjoyment from vocalizing. Normal babies have started babbling by the age of six months. The deaf child babbles, too, and his tones and sounds are very much like those of a normal child. If one did not know, it would be impossible to tell the differences between the two. However, the deaf child is not imitating the voices of others; he is merely engaging in chance vocalizations. Ewing (1958) states that at about the ninth month the hearing child will probably look up when he hears his name and also responds to a few other words. It is here that the deaf child really begins to fall behind in his development. The hearing child begins to understand words and obey them, but the deaf child can only imitate gestures.

A deaf child's parents need not wait until the child fails to talk to discover that he is deaf. There are many other ways to discover this. The parents can talk or make noises at different distances behind the child to see if he responds. If they suspect that the child does have impaired hearing they should take him to an otologist. The otologist can test the child for hearing loss as early as seven months of age. It is stated by Ewing (1958) that in severely deaf children, research has found that most of them drag their feet and are very clumsy. They tend to sit up and walk later than ordinary children do.

When parents discover they have a deaf child, they must accept the fact that the child is to be treated as much like a normal child as possible. Perhaps the only good thing about the parents not discovering their child's deafness at an early age is that they treat him as normal when they think that he is normal. The more normally the child is treated, the better adjusted he and his family will be. It is difficult for the parent to accept the fact that only in very few cases can the child's deficiency be cured.

Special procedures have been developed to teach deaf children to speak using the senses of touch, sight, and sound; but usually the child is two years old before he can be admitted to special schools. As soon as a parent discovers that his baby is deaf, he should immediately try to find out what can be done to help. Usually the parents can do a great deal to prepare the child for education, and in some cities, the deaf schools provide two-week courses for the parents of deaf children. If the parents do not live near such a school, home courses are available. Most parents need to overteach their children and forget that all the learning must take place in normal family-like situations. The teaching should be fun and the desire to communicate must be promoted. One of the best things that a parent can do is talk to the child in a pleasant tone using animated facial expressions.

The otologist, a medical doctor specializing in ear problems, can discover if the child has residual hearing. If he has, a hearing aid should be obtained as soon as possible and he should be taught how to use it to the fullest advantage. Frampton and Gall (1955) tell us that when talking to a deaf child a person should always get the child's attention and then talk directly facing him. The more the child is spoken to, the more he will want to respond in speech. Deaf children are more dependent upon their parents than hearing children and because of this the parents have extra responsibilities.

Preschool Education

Most authorities believe that if the deaf child learns to speak by parental training, he should be placed in an ordinary nursery or kindergarten. If he does not, he should be placed in a special nursery or day school for deaf children as soon as possible. By the time a deaf child finishes one of these schools, say Ewing and Ewing (1958), he should be able to enter an elementary school at about the same level of development as that of a hearing child. If the parents live in a rural district or small town, the child should be sent to a residential or boarding school for the deaf.

Authorities such as Ewing and Ewing (1958) tell us that the main aim of education for the deaf child is to give him words to think with, to understand the expressed thoughts of others, and to enable him to express his thoughts. They should be reached very early, and during these impressionable years must have their beginnings in communication established. Therefore they should be admitted to school at the earliest possible age.

In the nurseries, deaf children have routines similar to normal children except that special emphasis is placed on lipreading. We are told that after the child becomes familiar with the activities of the school, it becomes easy for him to recognize that certain movements of the teacher's lips must mean "Take off your coat," or "We're going out to play," because these are the things that have always happened at this time of the day. Thus we have the beginning of the child's lipreading. Now, with residual hearing, a hearing aid may be introduced. At first the child should wear it just a few minutes each day in order to hear a sound.

IDENTIFICATION

The school faces a great problem in trying to locate these children with hearing losses severe enough to warrant special help. The children are usually referred by the teacher. A group audiometric test is then given to those suspected of having a hearing loss. Another and better way is to give a group audiometric test to all children in the school system and refer those found to have a hearing loss to an otologist who will administer medical treatment if necessary.

Classification

The system of classification generally applied to the deaf is as follows:

1. The congenitally deaf—those born deaf.
2. The adventitiously deaf—those individuals who were born

with normal hearing but became deaf or nonfunctional later in life.

3. The hard-of-hearing—those individuals who have a functional sense of hearing with or without a hearing aid.

4. The profoundly deaf—those children who have a hearing loss greater than 75 decibels and who require intensive care and instruction without the use of a hearing aid.

5. The severely deaf—those children who have a hearing loss between 40 and 60 decibels and who need amplification of sounds for educational instruction.

6. Marginally deaf—those children having a 30 to 40 decibel loss in the better ear.

Prevalence

There is much conflict concerning prevalence, but according to Silverman (1957) 5 percent of school-age children have a hearing malfunction and roughly five in a thousand will require special attention educationally.

Measuring Hearing Loss

Although there are several crude, informal methods of testing hearing, including the Whisper Test, the Conversational Test, the Coin-Click Test, the Watch-Tick Test, and the Tuning-Fork Tests, the most accurate is made with a pure-tone audiometer.

Coin-Click and Watch-Tick

The Coin-Click Test consists of the administrator's dropping a large coin on a hard surface and clicking two small coins together. When the large coin, usually a half-dollar, is dropped on a hard surface the child is instructed to report whether he hears the coin ring or only a dull thud. If he hears only a thud it is presumed that he has a high-frequency hearing loss. If he hears the coin ring when it strikes the hard surface, it is presumed that his high-frequency hearing acuity is normal.

The administrator clicks two small coins together next to the subject's ear and asks the subject to inform him when he ceases to hear the clicks as the administrator backs away. From previous experience the administrator knows the distance at which the person with normal hearing can barely detect the click.

The Watch-Tick Test is administered in the same manner. The administrator must use the same watch at all times and a fairly noisy watch is preferred.

Conversational Test

The Conversational Test is administered at a distance of fifteen to twenty feet. The subject is placed at the prescribed distance from the examiner so that first one ear and then the other is tested. The examiner speaks numbers and words in a normal level of voice and asks the subject to repeat what he hears. If the subject is unable to repeat the words and numbers, the examiner moves toward him until he is able to repeat what the examiner is saying.

Tuning-Fork Tests

Tuning forks of various frequencies are selected for administering this test. This test is not an easy one to administer and should be done only by a physician. The most common tests are the Rinné, Weber, and Schwabach, named after their originators.

Pure-tone Audiometer

The pure-tone audiometer creates sounds of controlled intensity and frequency. *Frequency* is the number of vibrations per second of a given sound wave. *Intensity* is the loudness of the sound.

The individual responds when he hears a tone and the degree of hearing loss is recorded on an audiogram. The audiogram is marked by the examiner from −10 to 100 decibels and the hearing in each ear is tested and plotted separately (see Figs. 6-1 to 6-4).

Signs of Deafness in Children

If you answer "yes" to five of the following questions, then you, as a teacher or parent, should have the child tested using a pure-tone audiometer and refer him to an otologist if necessary.

1. Does he hear better when he is looking at you?

AUDIOGRAM

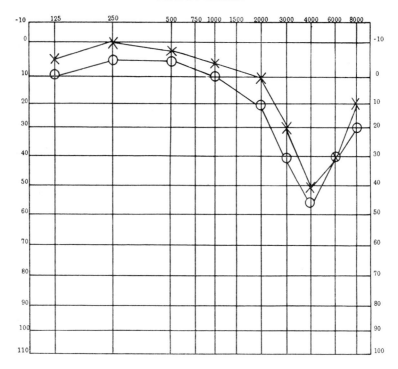

Sensory-Neural Impairment Resulting from Acoustic Trauma

FIGURE 6-1.

2. Does he turn T.V. up louder than you do?
3. Does he withdraw from people?
4. Does he respond to noises as opposed to words?
5. Does his voice have a monotonal quality?
6. Does he often have tantrums for attention getting?
7. Does he yell or scream to express pleasure?
8. Do his answers not make sense?

To Help the Child

The following is a list of ways in which parents and teachers can help the hearing-impaired child:

AUDIOGRAM

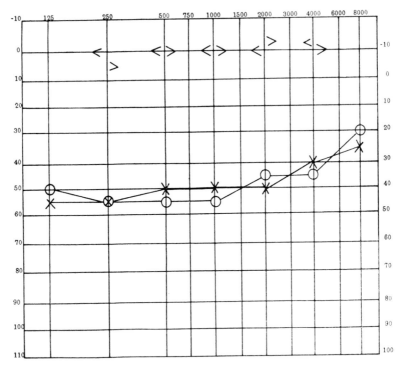

Typical Conductive Impairment

FIGURE 6-2.

1. Face him as you talk to him.
2. Have the child sit near the front of the room.
3. Talk naturally.
4. Ask the child to repeat directions.
5. Write out difficult and unusual words.
6. Place the child with his back to the light.

Types of Defects

There are three main types of defects:

1. Conductive hearing loss—the intensity of sound reaching the middle ear is reduced.

AUDIOGRAM

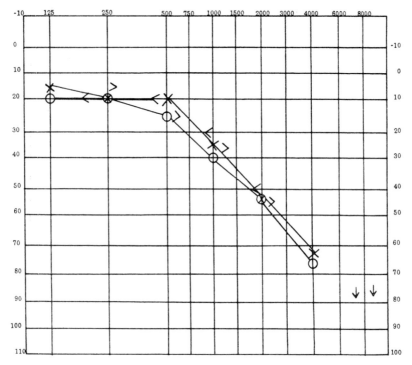

Typical Sensory-Neural Impairment

FIGURE 6-3.

2. Sensory-neural-defect—defect of the inner ear and of the transmitting auditory nerve.

3. Central deafness—hearing malfunction due to injury or abnormality of the central nervous system.

How We Hear

In Figure 6-5, there is a simplified description of how sound waves striking the ear drum operate the three smallest bones of the body (the ossicles—known as the hammer, anvil, and stirrup).

The stirrup, in turn, vibrates the oval window, a thin membrane stretched across the entrance to the inner ear. Movement of the oval window is passed on to the cochlea, the organ of

AUDIOGRAM

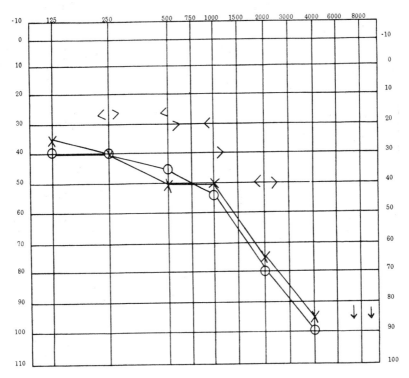

Typical Mixed Impairment

FIGURE 6-4.

hearing which "feels" the mechanical movements caused by the sound waves. This vibrating membrane, containing 25,000 tiny, hair-like cells, analyzes the vibrations received and sends the results to the brain via the eighth or hearing nerve.

Education of the Deaf

The two methods commonly used for the education of the deaf in institutions and special schools are referred to as oralism and manualism. The oral method does not use signs or gestures in developing speech but only uses speech and lipreading. The manual method uses gestures and the manual alphabet to achieve communication.

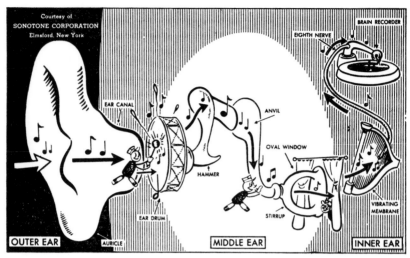

FIGURE 6-5.

There is much controversy concerning the education of the deaf. People involved usually classify themselves in one of the two stated categories, oralism and manualism. This controversy has been raging for many years, however, and evidently the years have not dimmed the beliefs or ardor of the two groups, they are still divided into opposing camps.

HISTORY

Certainly education for the deaf and hard-of-hearing is not a new concept. As early as 1550, oral education was provided for the deaf children of the nobility. In 1620 the first book concerning the deaf was written by Juan Pablo Bonet. Bonet's pupils were taught articulation and language of signs; therefore Bonet is known as the originator of the manual alphabet.

In the middle of the seventeenth century, Jacob Rodrigues Pereire extended Bonet's alphabet and introduced the sign language. Even more important, Pereire extended lipreading.

Abbé Charles Michel de l'Eppe founded the first public school for the deaf in 1775 in Paris. Abbé de l'Eppe believed that only by means of signs could the deaf be taught. A German contemporary, Samuel Heinicke, believed the deaf could learn to read lips and be taught to speak. Thomas Braidwood, of the British Isles, opened a school for the deaf in 1760 and used the oral method. An American, Thomas Hopkins Gallaudet, went to England to study the successful oral approach of Braidwood, but because of the secretive attitude of the Englishman, he had to go to France to study educational methods for the deaf. Gallaudet studied in France under Sicard, de l'Eppe's successor, and brought the manual approach to America.

First American School

The first school for the deaf in the United States was established at Hartford, Connecticut, in 1816 by Thomas Gallaudet. When it was opened for instruction, the first seven pupils were taught by the manual method. Gallaudet's work was later carried on by his son, Edward Minor Gallaudet, and today the federally sponsored college for the deaf in Washington, D. C., bears the name of the Gallaudets.

Gallaudet College offers the B.A., B.S., and M.S.E. degrees and allows only deaf youth to enter. Riverside City College in California offers deaf students a two-year program with emphasis in vocational subjects, but includes other college subjects such as English, psychology, history, etc. In 1966 the first Catholic institution for the deaf, St. Joseph College for the Deaf, was opened in Buffalo, New York.

CHARACTERISTICS OF THE HEARING-IMPAIRED

Many authorities believe that the Binet Intelligence Scale is unsuited for testing the deaf because of the language deficiency of these people. Therefore men like Pintner (1941) surveyed the results of other tests and concluded that the average IQ of the deaf is not quite 90. Myklebust (1960) bases his decisions and discussions concerning the deaf on more than twenty years of study. He found that the deaf, as a group, score higher on certain intelligence-test tasks than normal children and lower on certain others. Myklebust (1960) concludes that deafness affects intelligence more in the verbal areas than in the others.

Achievement

Pintner, Eisenson, and Stanton (1941), in their research, found no difference in the achievement of children who lost their hearing between two and five and those who lost it before the age of two. However, it is stated by Myklebust (1960) that children who lost their hearing after age six have a better concept of language than those losing it before six.

Fusfield (1954) studied the scores of the applicants to Gallaudet College on the Stanford Achievement Test and concluded that students did better in punctuation, capitalization, and grammar than in word and paragraph meaning.

A vocabulary study was conducted by Young and McConnell (1957), and they found that the hard-of-hearing child does not measure up to his intellectual capacity. In other words his scholastic achievement does not keep pace with his mental ability.

Adjustment

The impact of an impairment such as deafness depends upon the degree of deafness and the age of onset. If a child does not lose his hearing until age twelve or thirteen, he has acquired speech and the effect upon his development would not be as great as it would be upon the child born deaf or who loses his hearing before learning to talk. The prelanguage deaf child will not have normal experiences and is very limited in communications and social experiences. Pintner and Brunschwig (1936) found deaf children who come from families with no other deaf members are less well adjusted than deaf children from families with other deaf members.

If the schools and homes make unrealistic demands on the deaf children, the experience can lead to very disturbing problems for the children. Most authorities agree that if we do not try to make deaf children perform beyond their capacity they, as a group, are fairly well adjusted individuals.

Educational Provisions

Both the oral and manual methods are used in the education of the deaf in the U. S. today. In some schools a combined oral and manual approach is used and the program is fitted to the needs of the child.

In the *day school,* the child remains at home with his parents but attends the day school for instruction. All the children at the school are deaf. A *residential school* is a total program of training with cottage parents and education for the child. In *special classes,* children are grouped together according to age, ability, and interests. In *regular classes,* the hearing-impaired child attends a regular school and his special problems are handled by a regular class teacher.

The child should go to a regular class, special class, or day school if adequate provisions exist in the community. In many instances, the community does not have adequate facilities; therefore the child should go to a residential school.

There are several factors which influence whether a child can be educated in a regular class or a special facility. Naturally, intelligence is a factor as is the degree of deafness and the age of onset of deafness. The hard-of-hearing child of average or above intelligence should be able to function adequately in the regular classroom. The child who loses his hearing at age six or seven is far advanced in language development when compared to the child who is born deaf; nevertheless if he is profoundly deaf he may need institutional education.

Authorities in the field of education for the deaf emphasize acquisition of language as the greatest problem. The deaf child cannot acquire language from the spoken word as does the normal child. He is born in a society which was formed and fashioned by the influence of the spoken word through ages of development. The spoken word is the main influence from which the normal course of mental and social development stems. The normal child acquires language with ease and it becomes his passport into the society of which he is a part. As he becomes proficient in the use of language, he finds it increasingly easy to break through barriers that have separated him from other minds.

The deaf child does not acquire his passport to meaningful communication with others in this spontaneous way nor with the ease of the normal child. Language acquisition must be slowly and carefully structured by sequential steps before the deaf child can learn it and incorporate it into his intellectual frame of reference. Henry Ward Beecher said:

> Thinking cannot be clear till it has had expression.
> We must write, or speak, or act our thoughts, or they will remain
>   in a half torpid form.
> Our feelings must have expression, or they will be as clouds, which,
>   till they descend in rain, will never bring up fruit or flowers.
> So it is with all the inward feelings: expression gives them develop-
>   ment.
> Thought is the blossom; language the opening bud; action the fruit
>   behind it (Brown, 1965, p. 340).

Myklebust clearly described how a sensory deprivation such as deafness could limit the world of experience:

> It deprives the organism of some of the material resources from
> which the mind develops. Because total experience is reduced, there
> is an imposition on the balances and equilibrium of all psychologic
> processes. A lack of one type of sensation alters the integration and
> function of all the other types. Experience is therefore constituted
> differently; the world of perception, conception, imagination and
> thought has an altered foundation, a new configuration (McHugh,
> 1964, p. 386).

A recent report by the Advisory Committee on the Deaf to the Secretary of Health, Education, and Welfare (1965) outlines some of the shortcomings in the field of deaf education:

> The American people have no reason to be satisfied with their
> limited success in educating deaf children and preparing them for
> full participation in our society.
> Less than half of the deaf children needing specialized preschool
> instruction are receiving it.
> The average graduate of a public residential school for the deaf—
> the closest we have to generally available "high schools" for the
> deaf—has an eighth grade education.
> Seniors at Gallaudet College, the nation's only college for the
> deaf, rank close to the bottom in performance on the Graduate
> Record Examination.
> Five-sixths of our deaf adults work in manual jobs, as contrasted
> to only one-half of our hearing population.

This lack of development of the intellectual potential of the deaf is attributed to the lack of adequacy in the use of language.

This problem is summed up editorially by an authority in the field of education of the deaf:

> As educators of the deaf, we must never cease to seek and try new methods. We must be equally ruthless at discarding methods that do not stand the test. The test? Does it impart language to the deaf child? If it does not, it is not doing the job. No amount of bombast or argument can go around this basic problem, language. Give the deaf the ability to communicate intelligently and he will take it from there—the jet age, the space age, or any "you name it" are yet to come, notwithstanding (Fusfield, 1966, pp. 241-43).

As proof that other authorities in the area of education of the deaf are aware of acquisition of language as the crucial problem in educating the deaf child, the following is a thought on this theme that cuts through the basic structure of traditional education of the deaf:

> The history of the education of the deaf is full of sporadic suggestions to solve the problems. Let's face it—the real problem is lack of language. The person with good language, communicative skill, is having no problems of receiving adequate training and placement. Very seldom he or she has need of counseling and guidance.
>
> Given a well trained teacher for every deaf child, we face a problem of time distribution. Perhaps it would be wiser to devote more time to language—communicative skill—oral and written and less time to vocational work. This would mean a change of thinking on the part of administrators, teachers, parents, and the general public. The residential schools have been looked upon as terminal. This would no longer be true if we changed the emphasis to academic rather than a combination of academic and vocational. If we were to accept the concept of change in emphasis, we would need to make provision for vocational training on a post-graduate level, or dropout level (Fusfield, 1966, pp. 242-43).

Clearly language is crucial in the development of the intellectual growth of a child with deafness as a disability. Language, like amber, embalms and preserves the history and ancient wisdom of the world into which the deaf child is born. His socialization and ultimate self-actualization depends to a great degree upon his acquisition of language. He must become as competent in the use of language as his potentialities permit if he is to achieve a high degree of self-realization.

The Changing Population

On the changing population of the residential schools for the deaf that implied curriculum revision, Brill (1963) stated that there was a larger population of children identified as congenitally deaf. In addition to this, Weir (1963) noted the sharp increase in the number of multi-handicapped children in residential schools.

Another factor in the changing population of the residential school for the deaf is the emphasis on nursery and preschool programs. Statistics compiled by the *American Annals of the Deaf* (Doctor, 1960; 1964) revealed an average minimum age of admittance of 3.9 in 1960 and 3.5 in 1964. This shift in population calls for decisive curriculum in order to meet the needs of the children.

Another trend as revealed in current literature is in the area of vocational education. Williams (Ott, 1964) felt that vocational training as such is neither desirable nor possible in the present schools for the deaf. This, he feels, is because vocational education is highly specific and terminal.

Teaching Machines

Teaching machines to aid the deaf have been studied by researchers. Birch and Stuckless (1962) compared experimental and control groups of deaf children on a programmed approach to written language. They reported no difference between the groups in language learned, but stated that the experimental group learned the material in half the time. Fehr (1962) found favorable results in an experiment involving the teaching of language principles by a programmed approach.

New and improved training equipment available since World War II and the research involving such equipment is of importance to those in charge of curriculum planning. A recent development is a unisensory approach to auditory training known as acoupedics that appears to be of importance. Pollack (1964) described an acoupedics program as one which emphasized listening as a continuous activity which keeps an individual in constant contact with the world about him. This program departed from the multi-sensory approach by avoiding lipreading. Pollack reported that vocabulary is built more rapidly than for the visually oriented child; the voice quality is more pleasing; and speech patterns are more normal. This approach is limited to children with at least limited-hearing ability.

The need for continued research to improve education for all children, and for encouragement of the classroom teacher to try new ways of doing old things, was expressed recently by a teacher in the field of special education. She emphasized the use of all that has been successful in education since the dawn of history, but warned that among educators there is too much of a tendency to "follow the beaten path." She stated that mankind is only seeing the dawn of the new day that could come in the education of deaf children. She warned against too much conformity in schools in general and special education in particular. She suggested that education for exceptional children might be made better if educators got out of the rut of educational conformity and security in the familiar, and gave much thought to new methods and ideas that might help children to learn. She recalled the comment of Thoreau in "Walden" in which he said, "If a man does not keep pace with his companions, perhaps it is because he hears a different drummer. Let him step to the music that he hears however measured and far away." It might be in this way, she said, that the greatest advances would be made in the education of all children, and particularly the deaf child.

Legislation for the Deaf

Parents of deaf children will be interested in the following information from Hoag (1965):

> On June 8, 1965, President Johnson signed into law an act to provide for the establishment and operation of a National Technical Institute for the Deaf (Public Law 89-36). The legislation authorizes the Secretary of Health, Education, and Welfare to enter into an agreement with an institution of higher education for the establishment, construction, equipment, and operation of a post-secondary technical training facility for young deaf adults. A 12-member ad hoc National Advisory Board on the establishment of the National

Technical Institute for the Deaf will be appointed by the Secretary of Health, Education, and Welfare to review proposals from institutions of higher education and to advise him on location of the institute.

Early Guidance for the Parents

In an effort to secure positive attitudes in the parents, it is good to begin working with and guiding them while the child is still very young. It is obvious that attitudes can best be influenced while they are in the making.

There are three reasons why special problems exist for the deaf child. These special problems create a need for special services and help. The first reason is that parents, like others, have preconceived ideas about deafness which, unfortunately, are mostly quite negative. People think that loss of hearing incapacitates the individual and makes him helpless and dependent.

The second reason is that all parents expect their child to be at least normal and hope that he will be superior. If the body image of the child differs so radically from the one expected by the parents, they have to make a very painful and difficult adjustment. It is natural that they will blame themselves for the child's deafness, regardless of the truth. They feel that they have failed their child physically and will look for reasons for this imagined failure. Religious influences and naive concepts of justice as well as superstitions explain deafness as retribution for the sins committed by the parents. Thus many parents feel that deafness in their child is a punishment imposed upon them and are ashamed of their handicapped offspring.

The third and final reason is that as the child grows up, parents will be confronted with the effects of deafness on the child, most frequently in terms of slowing down his development and rate of learning. Parents expect their child to perform according to the standards set forth for other children. It is only natural that a deaf child will, in many instances, be unable to fulfill this expectation and will demand of the parents adjustments in treatment and techniques which are sometimes quite difficult.

When we consider that the above-mentioned things are true and that they greatly affect the handicapped child's functioning ability in society, then we understand that early guidance and counseling for the parent is a must. Many parents who are confronted with a hearing-impaired child are overwhelmed for lack of understanding concerning what they can and should do. The John Tracy Clinic offers two means by which parents can learn about their hard-of-hearing child. This clinic offers a correspondence course and has films available for parents.

The Alexander Graham Bell Association for the Deaf issues kits of literature dealing with the problems and needs of hearing-impaired children. The Conference of Executives of American Schools for the Deaf issues the same kind of kits mentioned above. Also, the American Hearing Society offers help for parents of hearing-impaired children through its local societies.

Resource Rooms

The hearing-impaired child needs the help of a resource teacher to help with certain academic subjects. In small towns, though, the resource room is out of the question. Many people must work together if the hearing-impaired child is to function adequately in the regular classroom. Parents, teachers, administrators, and other agencies must correlate their efforts in the best educational interests of the child.

This chapter does not deal with the child who is born deaf. If one is born profoundly deaf he must have special treatment and special placement in order to develop his maximum potential. Even with adequate placement few profoundly deaf children develop their maximum potential. In mentioning above that this chapter does not deal with the child who is born profoundly deaf, it is meant so far as educational placement in a regular classroom is concerned.

The hearing-impaired child faces many tasks and many conflicts. If he is to survive in the regular classroom he must have a great deal of help. He can be educated adequately, though, with help—and in the regular classroom.

REFERENCES
Advisory Committee on the Education of the Deaf: *Education of the Deaf: A Report to the Secretary of Health, Education, and Welfare.* U. S. Department of Health, Education, and Welfare, 1965.

Birch, Jack, and Stuckless, E. Ross: *The Development and Evaluation of Programmed Instruction in Language for Children with Auditory Disorders.* Pittsburgh, University of Pittsburgh, 1962.

Brill, Richard G.: Deafness and the genetic factor. *American Annals of the Deaf, 108:4,* 1963.

Brown, Ralph Emerson (Ed.): *The New Dictionary of Thoughts.* New York, Standard Book Company, 1965.

Doctor, Powrie V. (Ed.): *American Annals of the Deaf, 105,* 1960.

Doctor, Powrie V. (Ed.): *American Annals of the Deaf, 109,* 1964.

Ewing, Irene R., and Ewing, Alex W. G.: *New Opportunities for Deaf Children.* Springfield, Thomas, 1958.

Fehr, Joann D.: Programming language for deaf children. *Volta Review, 64,* 1962.

Frampton, Merle E., and Gall, Elena D.: *Special Education for the Exceptional.* Boston, Porter Sargent, 1955, Vol. I.

Fusfield, Irving S.: A Cross Section Evaluation of the Academic Program of Schools for the Deaf. Gallaudet College Bulletin, 1954.

Fusfield, Irving S.: Guidelines for the langauge teaching program. *Report of the Proceedings of the Forty-Second Meeting of American Instructors of the Deaf.* U. S. Government Printing Office, Document 71, 1966.

Hoag, Ralph L.: National technical institute for the deaf. *Exceptional Children, 32,* 1965.

McHugh, Hollie, M.D., C.M.: Sensorineural deafness in children. *Report of the Proceedings of the Forty-First International Congress on Education of the Deaf.* U. S. Government Printing Office, Document 106, 1964.

Myklebust, Helmer R.: *The Psychology of Deafness.* New York, Grune & Stratton, 1960.

Ott, Joseph T. (Ed.): *Proceedings of a National Workshop on Improved Vocational Opportunities for the Deaf.* Knoxville, University of Tennessee, 1964.

Pintner, R., and Brunschwig: Some personality adjustments of deaf children in relation to two different factors. *Journal of Genetic Psychology, 49,* 1963.

Pintner, Rudolph; Eisenson, Jon, and Stanton, Mildred: *The Psychology of the Physically Handicapped.* New York, F. S. Crofts and Company, 1941.

Pollack, Doreen: Acoupedics: A uni-sensory approach to auditory training. *Volta Review, 66,* 1964.

Silvermen, Richard: Education of the deaf. Travis, Lee E. (Ed.): *Handbook of Speech Pathology.* New York, Appleton-Century-Crofts, 1957.

Weir, R. C.: The impact of the multiple handicapped on special education. *Volta Review, 65*:6, 1963.

Wooden, Harley Z.: Deaf and hard of hearing children. In Dunn, Lloyd M.: *Exceptional Children in the Schools.* New York, Holt, Rinehart and Winston, 1963.

Young, C., and McConnell, F.: Retardation of vocabulary development in hard of hearing children. *Exceptional Children, 23,* 1957.

Chapter 7

THE PHYSICALLY HANDICAPPED CHILD
IN THE REGULAR CLASSROOM

P HYSICALLY HANDICAPPING conditions have existed since the advent of man, and the human race has had the problem of dealing with those not endowed with the ability to function in society as most so-called normal people. One may define orthopedic handicaps as defects which cause interference with normal use of bones, muscles, or joints; the condition may be congenital or it may be due to disease or an accident. Some of the conditions included in the term "orthopedic handicaps" are muscular dystrophy, multiple sclerosis, poliomyelitis, spina bifida, cerebral palsy, club foot, congenital dislocation of the hip, scoliosis, skeletal deformities, bone cysts and tumors, and many other conditions caused by accidents.

EDUCATION

The physically handicapped were first found in the regular classes. Later they were taken out and educated in institutions, day schools, and the like, as was the trend in America during the 1960's; but the present trend is to place as many as possible back into the regular classes where they can benefit from equal educational opportunities.

There are many variables to be considered when determining whether to place the physically handicapped in the regular classes. Frances P. Conner (cited in Cruickshank and Johnson, 1958) says essentially, "Children with motor disabilities are not very different from others." This is true.

The orthopedically handicapped child is the least difficult to absorb within a regular group (Leeper, Dales, Skipper,

Witherspoon, 1968). However, the crippling defect must be minor or special provision needs to be made for handling the child. This special provision can be made in the regular classroom though.

Leta S. Hollingworth (1925) makes a pertinent statement:

> In all generations there has never been another just like anyone, and there will never be exactly his like again. So far from being irritated by the idiosyncracies of our own fellows, we ought to cherish this variety as a thing that makes life worth living. Instead of striving to force all children to learn the same things in the same way . . . we ought to foster individuality in its socially valuable aspects, so that the charm of human contact may be increased.

These children require much assistance, which should be given in such a way that it is not resented. Children with physical disabilities are usually retarded socially and emotionally, which could cause added problems in a regular classroom (Cruickshank and Johnson, 1958). Teachers must adapt the regular program of education to fit the needs of the physically handicapped children. Individualized instruction needs to be used to its fullest potential. Kirk and Weiner (1963), on the other hand, feel that the educational management of the physically handicapped requires school plant changes and alterations in physical arrangements rather than special teaching techniques.

Once a physically handicapped child is placed in a regular class, much follow-up work needs to be included. The school should be in contact with agencies that have training available for those students not able to further their education, and which will enable those unable to go to college to prepare themselves for some type of employment.

Programs for the Physically Handicapped

Programs for the physically handicapped have not been increasing as much as programs for many other exceptionalities have. These programs are not even increasing at the same rate as the total public school enrollment. This is probably due to an increasing trend to provide for more physically handicapped children in regular classes.

In the special class the provisions which have to be made are usually for physical rather than academic reasons. There is usually a heterogeneity of crippling conditions in one of these classes. One child may be crippled in one arm, another in both arms, but not in the legs, and another in both legs but not in the arms. One may be mobile in the classroom, another may be mobile on crutches, and another may be confined to a wheel-chair. There is often a wide range of chronological and mental age levels. This is not good and is found more often in smaller communities where there are only a few crippled children in the school system. The issue which should be considered is whether education is enhanced by the adaptation of the physical surroundings rather than the devising of special methods of teaching. If a child is unable to hold his book or to write because of a physical handicap, it becomes necessary to develop devices which aid him in holding a book or communicating on paper. This, however, can be done in the regular classroom.

Too frequently, the school has placed a physically handi-capped child in a special facility, away from his peer group, and then bragged about the wonderful program for crippled children. Some physically handicapped children do need a separate school program and a modified school facility; however this is not true for the majority of physically handicapped children.

CEREBRAL PALSY

The condition now known as cerebral palsy has existed as far back as recorded history goes, as noted in biblical descrip-tions of the lame and in ancient Egyptian hieroglyphics depicting the characteristic postures of the cerebral palsied. The earliest references to the relationship between intracranial hemorrhage at birth and the later development of cerebral palsy can be found in medical literature dated 1826 to 1835. In 1838 a London orthopedist, William John Little, described some of the con-sequences of birth lesions, and in 1869 gave the name "spastic paralysis" to the condition characterized by a cross-legged gait, drooling, speech difficulties, and mental retardation. The condi-tion became known as "Little's disease" and his belief that the prognosis for those so afflicted was hopeless persisted for many years.

In the early 1900's, during an epidemic of poliomyelitis, it was discovered that many children being brought to clinics diagnosed as victims of infantile paralysis actually had "Little's disease." The problem was thus forced to the attention of the medical profession. Many doctors began to question Little's "hopeless" attitude and launched full-scale investigations into the problem. Among these pioneers were Bronson Crothers and one of his students, Winthrop Morgan Phelps, both physicians. Phelps is given credit for proposing the term "cerebral palsy." "Cerebral" denotes that the causative lesion is in the brain; "palsy" indicates the consequence of such a lesion, which is a loss of, or impaired, motor functioning.

During the last ten years cerebral palsy has become an increasingly familiar term to many professions and the general public as a result of increased research, educational and fund-raising campaigns, and the active parent groups which have been organized in all parts of the country. We are told that there is one cerebral palsied individual born per every 215 live births, or seven cerebral palsied births per 100,000 of our population, or one cerebral palsied birth every fifty-three minutes. The medical profession is keeping these babies alive and promising them an increased life expectancy every day. But what happens to the families who must make room for a handicapped child, the schools which must educate them, the industries which will be asked to hire them, and the society which will be asked to accept them? Behind the statistics are human beings. Interest in the complexities of cerebral palsy and the details of its prevention and treatment must always be oriented toward the individual. In order that these individuals can learn to function to the highest level of their capacities, the combined efforts of the medical profession, the psychologists, the teachers, the speech, occupational, and vocational therapists, and many others are necessary.

Cerebral palsy has aroused public interest and concern in recent years; it is a major medical and sociological problem; but many people do not realize the complexity of this condition.

Perlstein (1959) defines cerebral palsy as ". . . a condition characterized by paralysis, paresis, incoordination, dyskinesia, or aberration of motor function that is due to involvement of the motor areas of the brain" (pp. 30-34). In addition to the motor dysfunction there are usually coexisting conditions such as mental retardation, sensory loss, convulsions, and emotional disturbances. Crothers and Paine (1959) point out that two arbitrary criteria have been generally accepted: the lesion must occur in early life, and no progressive disease may exist at the time of the diagnosis.

Cerebral palsy has been defined in the United Cerebral Palsy Research and Educational Foundation Program for Calendar Year 1961 as follows:

> Cerebral palsy is the clinical picture, usually manifesting itself in childhood, with dysfunction of the brain in which one of the major components is motor disturbance.
>
> Thus, cerebral palsy may be described as a group of conditions, usually originating in childhood, characterized by paralysis, weakness, incoordination or any other aberration of motor function caused by pathology of the motor control centers of the brain. In addition to such motor dysfunction, cerebral palsy may include learning difficulties, psychological problems, sensory defects, convulsions and behavioral disorders of organic origin (Phelps, 1950).

Incidence

There are many different estimates on the number of cerebral palsy victims. Phelps (1950) reported that seven afflicted children were born each year per 100,000 population. He states that one of these children would die during infancy, which would change the estimate to six per 100,000 population. Recent figures given by the United Cerebral Palsy Associations estimate the number of cerebral palsied individuals at 550,000. This is an even larger number than the projected figures of Phelps' study. Cardwell (1956) suggests the increased birthrate may be the reason for the difference.

Etiology

The causative factors of cerebral palsy may be divided into three main groups: prenatal, natal, and postnatal.

Prenatal Factors

Causative factors existing prior to birth include the following:

1. *Heredity.* Certain body defects may be transmitted through germ cells, and certain disorders occur in families with a better-than-chance frequency.

2. *Acquired in utero.*

a. *Prenatal infections.* Measles, mumps, syphilis, and maternal poisons can all affect the fetus.

b. *Prenatal anoxia.* This can be the result of maternal anemia, cord anomalies, and the premature separation of the cord.

c. *Prenatal cerebral hemorrhage.* Hemorrhage may result from direct trauma, blood conditions of the mother, and other causes.

d. *Metabolic disturbances.* Irradiation may produce changes in the fetus.

e. *Developmental anomalies* caused by drugs.

Natal Factors

Conditions at birth, such as the ones listed below, may also be causative factors.

1. *Anoxia.* Anoxia may be due to placenta separation, breech delivery, and many other causes. The basal ganglia is most sensitive to oxygen deprivation and lesions in this area sometimes result in athetosis.

2. *Trauma and hemorrhage.* Cerebral damage may result from prolonged labor, sudden pressure changes, precipitate delivery, Caesarean delivery, and malpositions.

3. *Constitutional.*

a. *Prematurity. Illingworth* (1958) states that one third of all cerebral palsied children are born prematurely. Brenda (1952) believes that hemorrhage and asphyxiation are more apt to occur because of the inadequate development of the blood vessels. The premature child may also be anemic and have a lowered resistance to infection. Some brain damage may be caused by prematurity, but the child may be born early because there is an existing abnormality. Tizard (1955) states that it is known that abnormal fetuses tend to be expelled early, and he suggests that in some cases prematurity is the result rather than the cause of the abnormality.

b. *Rh incompatibility.* Rh incompatibility refers to a state in which, due to the incompatibility of the blood types of the mother and father of a child, the child's blood type, if it is inherited from the father, is incompatible with the mother's. Incompatibility occurs only when the mother's Rh type is negative and the child's is positive.

Postnatal Factors

The following are causative factors which may develop after birth:

1. *Trauma.* Cerebral palsy may develop from accidental blows to the brain, skull fractures, and other head wounds.

2. *Infections.* Meningitis, encephalitis, and brain abscess often cause cerebral damage. Post infectious and postimmunization encephalomyelitis are reported by Illingworth (1958) as factors in cerebral palsy.

3. *Toxic agents.* Arsenic, lead, coal-tar derivates and carbon monoxide gas are believed to cause cerebral damage.

4. *Vascular.* Injury may result from sudden pressure changes.

5. *Anoxia.* Illingworth (1958) states that anoxia may result from strangulation or carbon monoxide poisoning.

6. *Neoplasms.* This group includes brain tumors and cysts. No condition in which a progressive brain lesion is present can be classified as cerebral palsy, but the residual effects of the lesion are included as cerebral palsy.

There are many causes of cerebral palsy but Denhoff (1955) believes that the common denominator is lack of oxygen associated with genetic, mechanical, infectious, and metabolic conditions. Denhoff adds that there is some evidence that maternal constitutional factors may make the difference between the children who are brain-damaged from lack of oxygen and the children who escape damage.

Physiological Pathology

The various manifestations of cerebral palsy are produced by lesions in certain areas of the brain. Failure of development, injury, anoxia, hemorrhage, or degeneration may cause loss of brain cells. Tizard (1955) points out that there can be no regeneration of the lost cells, so the anatomical defects are permanent. This is an area in which much research is being done, and this statement may not be correct in a few years.

The type of motor dysfunction depends on the region in which the damage occurs. Perlstein (1952) and others have classified the types of involvement by the site of the anatomical lesion.

Physiological Classification

Discussed below are the three classifications of cerebral palsy: spasticity, dyskinesia, and ataxia. Within these classifications, specific types have been distinguished.

Spasticity

Spasticity is characterized by the presence of the stretch reflex, which is the principal diagnostic sign of this type. Other findings are an exaggeration of the deep tendon reflexes, and ankle clonus. This class composes approximately 60 percent of all cerebral palsy cases. Muscle movements are explosive, jerky, or poorly performed.

The *stretch reflex* is described by Perlstein (1952):

> . . . an increased tendency of the muscle to contract when passively stretched rapidly. This reflex is not present when the muscle is passively stretched slowly. The stretch reflex is not limited to the stretched muscle alone, but tends to spread to contiguous muscles, with the result that a mass motion of the whole extremity may occur . . . The stretch reflex is more commonly found in the antigravity muscles . . .

Perlstein (1952) referred to *ankle clonus* as another diagnostic sign frequently observed in spasticity. It is characterized by a "cog-wheel" type of jerking reaction brought about by a sudden and forceful flexion, or bending of the foot back toward the leg.

The *hyperactive knee jerk,* characteristic of the spastic, is stimulated by tapping the tendon just below the knee cap while the person being examined sits on the table with his thigh supported but his lower leg hanging from the table. When this reflex is present the lower leg jerks forcefully upward.

Convulsions and mental retardation may be present in many cases. It is believed by many authorities that the spastics with hand involvement are most likely to have seizures.

Dyskinesia

Three types of cerebral palsy that are grouped in this class are athetosis, rigidity, and tremor. Dyskinesia is characterized by an abnormal amount and type of motion. There is an abnormality in spontaneous motion which may be slow or rapid, constant or intermittent. Perlstein (1952) believes that several forms of dyskinesia may occur in the same child, one form predominating one day, another form the next day. There may be delayed postural development and retention of postural reflexes, such as the tonic neck reflex and the neck righting reflex.

Athetosis can involve one or all of the extremities as well as the muscles supplied by the cranial nerves. Attempted activities result in slow involuntary movements. The involuntary movements seem to disappear when the child sleeps, but they increase during conscious movement. Speech problems are common in athetosis and there is often a tendency to drool. Approximately 20 percent of all cases of cerebral palsy are in this diagnostic category. The most outstanding feature of the athetoid type is involuntary movements of the voluntary muscles of the trunk and extremities.

Denhoff (1955) states that motor activity in the *tremor* type of cerebral palsy may resemble athetoid movements, but the tremor is more rhythmic in character. He adds that the individuals affected have constant involuntary reactions. This condition is rare in children. Cases of cerebral palsy manifesting the tremor type of clinical picture, along with the next type of this disorder to be discussed, rigidity, comprise approximately 10 percent of all cases of cerebral palsy. It is obvious, therefore, that these are rather rare types.

The incidence of *rigidity* among cases of cerebral palsy has been discussed previously in connection with tremor. Cardwell (1956) asserted that in rigidity both the contracting muscles and their antagonists are affected; however, the antagonists are more severely involved which makes voluntary motions of the affected part of the body quite difficult. Attempts to move the involved area of the body in rigidity, this author stated, may be accompanied by involuntary movements of other areas. Individuals affected by this type of cerebral palsy are found by Cardwell to be mentally deficient more frequently than those manifesting spasticity or athetosis.

Ataxia

Ataxia is caused by lesions to the cerebellum and is characterized by a loss of balance. Sometimes there is a voluntary tremor. Guyton (1956) states that this tremor is much coarser than the tremor caused by lesions in the basal ganglia. This category does not occur as frequently as the spastic or athetoid group.

Topographical Classification

According to Perlstein (1952), topographical involvement may be classified in the following way:

1. Monoplegia—one limb involved. This is rare.
2. Paraplegia—involves the legs only and is usually the spastic type.
3. Hemiplegia—lateral one half of the body involving the hand and the leg. These types are usually spastic.
4. Triplegia—involves three extremities, usually the legs and an arm.
5. Quadriplegia—all four extremities are involved. The individuals may be spastic, rigid, or athetoid.
6. Diplegia—this involves both legs. There may be some hand involvement.
7. Double hemiplegia—this term indicates a quadriplegia in which the arms are more involved than the legs.

Incidence of Convulsions

Perlstein (1952) reported a close correlation between topographical classifications, educability, and the incidence of convulsions. He believes that the incidence of convulsions is greater where hand involvement is greater; for example, the incidence of convulsions in a paraplegic is apt to be less than in a quadriplegic.

Classification of Involvement

A widely accepted classification of cerebral palsy according to the severity of involvement is as follows:

Mild involvement. The individual is able to ambulate, use his arms and communicate well enough for his own needs.

Moderate involvement. The individual is affected enough to be handicapped in locomotion, self-help, and communication; but he is not totally disabled. He will require some special help.

Severe involvement. This individual is incapacitated and is usually confined to a wheelchair. Complete rehabilitation mav not be possible for these individuals.

Intelligence

Holden (1952) indicated the meager psychological studies concerning the cerebral palsied child, but noted the growing interest shown in psychological appraisal from 1947 to 1952. He stated the following:

> In the fifteen year period between 1931 and 1946 a total of 17 articles were reported, or an average of approximately one article per year. In contrast, in the five year period between 1947 and 1952, a total of 91 articles were reported, or an average of 18.2 articles per year (pp. 92-99).

A number of studies which were noted by Holden "indicated an incidence of mental deficiency of from 45 to 50 percent in cerebral palsied children, even when flexible test procedures were utilized." He suggested that future studies should treat separately the athetoid and spastic to test whether or not there are significant basic psychological differences between the two types of cerebral palsy.

Prognosis

The prognosis for individuals with cerebral palsy may only be stated in terms of percentages and broad group classifications which some authorities utilize in categorizing these individuals in relation to the achievements that might be expected of them. Although prognostic classifications are useful in theory, an accurate prognosis for any individual case is extremely difficult to make.

Therapy

Occupational, physical, and speech therapy will be briefly discussed because they are so vital to the education and/or habilitation or rehabilitation of cerebral palsied individuals. These three disciplines are utilized by other types of physical handcaps, too, but not to the extent that the cerebral palsied need them.

Occupational Therapy

HISTORY. Willard and Spackman (1957) stated that occupational therapy as a profession is relatively young, having had its beginning during the time of World War I. However, some of the underlying principles of occupational therapy have been recognized for centuries. Ancient records show that the Egyptians and the Greeks used music and games to assist the recovery of mental patients.

When hospitals were developing at the end of the eighteenth century and the beginning of the nineteenth century, a number of humanitarians began advocating and practicing the use of occupation for the restoration of mental health. Occupation was taken for some time to mean labor or sharing in the domestic work of the hospital. Gradually this type of work was supplemented with activity of a more diversionary and recreational nature.

By the early 1900's, the practice of employing craft teachers to work with patients became quite common in both public and private mental hospitals, and in 1908 a training course for such workers was offered by the Chicago School of Civics and Philanthropy. In 1917, a group of leaders in this field organized the National Society for the Promotion of Occupational Therapy, which later became the American Occupational Therapy Association.

DEFINITION. Dunton (1957) referred to Pattison, who defined

occupational therapy as "any activity, mental or physical, definitely prescribed and guided for the distinct purpose of contributing to and hastening recovery from disease or injury."

TRAINING AND QUALIFICATION IN OCCUPATIONAL THERAPY. Occupational therapy requires four years of college training leading to the degree of Bachelor of Science in Occupational Therapy. Thirty or more colleges and universities offering training in occupational therapy are accredited by the Council on Medical Education and Hospitals of the American Medical Association.

THE FUNCTION OF OCCUPATIONAL THERAPY. The functions of occupational therapy can be classified under four broad objectives: (1) physical restoration, (2) psychiatric integration, (3) psychological adjustment, and (4) prevocational evaluation. In the activities planned for the patient the therapist may be working for goals under one or more of these four groups at the same time.

Physical Therapy

According to Lethourneau (1955), physical therapy is the treatment of disease and injury by physical means such as heat, light, water, electricity, massage, and therapeutic exercise, but excluding treatment by x-ray and radioactive substances. The use of heat, electrotherapy, and hydrotherapy in the treatment of cerebral palsy has declined. Today most accepted therapeutic procedures place the patient in the role of the worker, with the therapist as foreman.

Physical therapy aids the cerebral palsied in achieving their total capabilities through the use of active, passive, and resistive exercises; by initiating normal joint-motion patterns; and by establishing balance and functional activities. Functional activities include walking, sitting, locking and unlocking the braces, and other activities of daily living.

HISTORY. The healing properties of heat, light, and water have been known since the dawn of history, and reference to them appears frequently in ancient writings. At the turn of the century, physical therapy was administered almost entirely by physicians, but competent nurses gradually assumed responsibility in this area, and the profession of physical therapy slowly evolved.

Although, theoretically, physical therapy is to be given upon specific directions of a physician, no prescription can be so specific as to provide for every event. So that the patient may receive maximum benefit from the therapy, such discretion must be left to the physical therapist.

The following are goals of the physical therapy program:

1. To become aware of how the physical therapist can help the classroom teacher.

2. To become aware of how classroom teachers can help the physical therapist.

3. To help the cerebral palsied individual take his place in society.

The ultimate aim of treatment is to help the cerebral palsied become as independent as their physical handicaps will allow. The treatment should help each person, insofar as possible, become personally, socially, and economically independent. In the more involved cases, the aim may be to reduce the amount of care needed.

Speech Defects

Van Riper (1954) states:

> . . . speech is defective when it deviates so far from the speech of other people that it calls attention to itself, interfers with communication, or causes its possessor to be maladjusted. This may be due to organic, environmental, or psychogenic factors, or by any combination of these three in a particular person.

Incidence of Speech Defects with Cerebral Palsy

There are more children of school age with speech defects than in any other area of exceptionality. In this group we find that the speech defects often accompany cerebral palsy. Mecham (1966) revealed that 70 to 80 percent of persons with cerebral palsy have some involvement of speech and/or hearing, often produced by the brain damage which has produced the cerebral palsy. Wolfe and Reid (1958) reported that 74.54 percent of the cerebral palsied children studied also have speech problems.

Characteristic Speech of Children with Cerebral Palsy

Because the speech problems in any other type of cerebral palsy are so diverse, it is almost impossible to describe a characteristic type of speech as cerebral palsy speech. Rutherford (1950) supports this by adding that speech is variable within the individual as well as within the group.

In a study by Denhoff and Holden (1960), it was found that spastics were more proficient in speech than athetoids. Wolfe (1958) found that almost 100 percent of the athetoids he studied had some involvement of the speech mechanism.

History of Speech Therapy with the Cerebral Palsied

Speech defects have been considered the same as other handicaps since time began. They have been treated as hopeless along with the retarded and the crippled. Therefore cerebral palsied children with speech defects have been rejected or destroyed, used as sources of entertainment, and treated with pity. Now we are beginning to see them as useful human beings. It is up to our society to remove a few of the obstacles which face every handicapped person. Speech defects are among these obstacles.

CONGENITAL DEFORMITIES

The chances are fifteen to one that when a baby is born he will be normal. In other words, for every fifteen normal children, one will be defective. The probability of a normal birth could be improved if existing knowledge were applied now and research pushed forward to help forestall the accidents of abnormalities at birth. These accidents cause approximately seven hundred babies to be born every day in the United States with defects serious enough to cause physical and/or mental handicaps.

Basic research in biological processes is providing clues to the causes of these abnormalities. Discovery is the first step toward development of prevention. Thus far there are no drugs or vaccines that can prevent congenital malformations. However, of significance today is the accumulation of knowledge concerning early diagnosis and treatment of the defects not yet prevented.

Fortunately a large majority of newborn babies are without serious abnormalities. Most babies are born with some kind of birth defect. Some are born color-blind; some are slightly pigeon-toed; others do not have good coordination. Almost everyone has a mole of some kind. These are minor and non-disabling defects.

Definition

A congenital deformity is a defect that is present at birth. These deformities can occur in any of the body systems and/or organs. Gross deformities, recognizable by anyone, include absence of an extremity and extra fingers or toes. Other conditions, which can be detected through a detailed study by a doctor include absence of part of the brain or malformations of the heart. The detection of an abnormality may not necessarily indicate the degree of disability which it may cause. A serious birth defect is one that can cause disfigurement, result in a physical or mental handicap, shorten life, or be fatal for the newborn baby. Birth defects are defined by the National Foundation for the March of Dimes (1969) as "structural or metabolic disorders present at birth, whether genetically determined or the result of environmental interference during embryonic or fetal life. Birth injuries are not included."

There are hundreds of birth defects. They may range from such deformities as open spine (spina bifida) which is apparent at birth, to other errors like diabetes which are often undetected until they cause mental or physical handicaps later in life (spina bifida and diabetes are covered in another chapter).

Incidence

An estimated 7 percent of all newborn chidren in the United States each year have defects evident at birth or detected during their first year of life. More than half a million deaths are caused each year by birth abnormalities. Approximately 500,000 still births, miscarriages, and spontaneous abortions are due to defects in the fetal development. An estimated 15 million Americans of all ages have one or more birth abnormalities which affect their lives daily.

Although birth defects are found in both males and females and in every race, deformities are more common in certain groups than in others. Extra fingers occur among Orientals more than Caucasians and even more often among Negroes. Malformations of the lips and mouth are prevalent in Caucasians rather than Negroes, and even more so among Orientals. Congenital dislocation of the hip occurs more often among females, while a narrowing of the pylorus (stomach opening into intestines) is more common among males.

Clubfoot

Clubfoot occurs in about one of every 250 births. The foot turns inward or outward and in a tip-toe position. The cause of a clubfoot may possibly be the position of the child in the uterus or malformation of the limb. Mild defects may be treated with shoe splints worn at night, along with simple braces or corrective shoes. The more serious clubfoot may be associated with other defects. This condition tends to recur, so muscles and ligaments must be stretched and bones realigned. Plastic casts can often correct this condition. Surgery may be necessary.

Congenital Urinary Tract Defects

Congenital urinary tract defects occur in one out of every 250 births. There are many types, involving kidneys, bladder, and genitalia. Organs may be fused, absent, or obstructed. Certain hormones given during pregnancy may cause these malformations. There may also be some hereditary tendencies. Most congenital urinary tract defects can be corrected by surgery.

Polydactyly

Polydactyly (a developmental anomaly characterized by extra fingers and toes) appears most often in Negro populations, occurring in one out of every 100, as opposed to one in 600 among white populations. Fused fingers and toes (syndactyly) have no racial variations. Causes of these conditions are unknown, but it is believed they may frequently be hereditary. The cure for polydactyly is simple amputation done at birth. Surgery is also necessary for syndactyly, to help improve the function of the fingers and toes. Usually the thumb and the big toe are first considered due to their necessity for grasping and balance respectively.

Congenital Amputees

Missing limbs are very rare in our society. Congenital amputees are those born without one to four of their limbs or with their limbs severely deformed. There are no known causes for congenital amputations, but the drug thalidomide, used by pregnant mothers to control nausea and in sleeping pills, is believed to be one causative factor. The use of prosthetic or artificial limbs and devices helps these children and their families adjust better. It also helps to relieve distressed emotional state which often accompanies this condition.

Scoliosis

Scoliosis is a condition characterized by lateral curvature of the spine. This condition may be congenital but is also acquired because of injuries, disease, or poor posture. About 19 out of every 1,000 of our population over the age of fourteen years have this disability to some degree. It is among the twenty most common conditions found in special education programs for nonsensorially physically handicapped children.

Congenital Hip Dislocation

Congenital dislocation of the hip is a defect in which the head of the femur is displaced in the hip socket. If this condition is not corrected, permanent crippling results. Early recognition and prompt correction of this condition has been successful to the extent that this abnormality is seldom seen in an adult person.

OTHER CAUSES OF PHYSICAL HANDICAPS
Poliomyelitis

Poliomyelitis is one of the most publicized of the weak-muscle diseases. As a consequence of this disease, paralysis of the muscles is evident. However, it is the nerve cells in the spinal cord which are damaged by the polio virus. There has been a significant reduction in postpolio paralysis cases by the use of polio vaccines which prevent paralysis in about 75 percent of the cases. Approximately 80 percent of the youngsters having polio can attend regular classes once the disease is under control.

Skeletal Deformities

Skeletal deformities in children affect primarily the upper and lower limbs, spine, and joints. Therefore a disability such as this may handicap a child in walking, standing, sitting, or using his hands. These conditions may be present at birth or acquired at a later date because of accidents, developmental disorders, or infectious diseases. The most common of the congenital types is a condition of the feet and ankles. Clubfoot, which is a condition involving one or both feet and characterized by the turning downward and inward of the ankles, accounts for 25 percent of congenital anomalies and 75 percent of crippling conditions involving the feet. Clubfoot is discussed earlier in this chapter.

Bone Cysts and Tumors

Bone cysts and tumors are causes of crippling conditions in children and should be mentioned in a chapter such as this. A bone cyst is usually a slow-growing, bone-destructive lesion located near one end of the shaft of a bone. Tumors of course are growths which may be benign or malignant. Parental attitudes are very important in the total picture of life in the home when a child has a malignant tumor. A parent who is constantly depressed will often cause other members of the household to be depressed too.

Muscular Dystrophy

Medical science has focused much effort on combating the problem of muscular dystrophy, but many individuals still have a pessimistic view of prevention and treatment for children who suffer from this affliction. The number of persons affected by muscular dystrophy is not known but the mortality rate involved includes more than 50 percent who are children between three and thirteen years of age.

Grouped under muscular dystrophy are disturbances of the skeletal musculature characterized by progressive loss of muscular strength and eventually involving the entire muscular system. This type of disturbance is perhaps the most seriously disabling condition of childhood because, unlike poliomyelitis or cerebral palsy, the child gradually becomes weaker and weaker, and the majority die of a respiratory disease early in life.

Although medical literature describes in detail the various signs and types of muscular dystrophy, very little can be found detailing the treatment involved. Because of the hopeless attitude expressed by so many authorities, these children have not been given the care they deserve and as a result have become hopelessly crippled.

At the onset of muscular dystrophy, the child can remain in the regular classroom while receiving the help of specialists who attempt to make his life as meaningful as possible. During the later stages of the condition, the child may need the services of an itinerant teacher, or he may be admitted to a hospital school. In some cases the child suffering from muscular dystrophy may be placed in a special class for the physically handicapped.

Multiple Sclerosis

Multiple sclerosis is a disease of the central nervous system and is more prevalent among young adults than among young children or adolescents. The onset of this condition is insidious. The first symptoms may be double vision, prickling sensations in the extremities, body tremors, speech difficulties, bladder involvement, nystagmus, coordination difficulties, or emotional disturbance. Multiple sclerosis is progressive and at present there is no cure. Temporary remissions during which there are no symptoms are common and must be considered in the overall program for an individual having this disease.

Not many young children will be affected by this disease;

therefore the educational system will not be too involved at the elementary level. Some high school students will have multiple sclerosis and even more college students; therefore the regular class teacher and college instructors will be involved in classroom management for this individual. At the high school level the teenager will be treated just like any other child at the onset of the disease, except in the case of strenuous exercise. Later, though, provisions must be made for a wheelchair and, eventually, home-bound teaching. The college student will follow about the same program as the high school student, but it will be more individualized according to the student's major emphasis.

Arthritis

The story of arthritis began millions of years ago when the dinosaurs walked the earth. We know these twenty-ton animals were victims of arthritis because their skeletons show many of their huge bones grown together as a result of the disease.

We get the name for this disease from two Greek words, "arthros" (joint) and "itis" (inflammation). Regular class teachers will have children in their classes who suffer from arthritis. The resultant swollen fingers, knees, and elbows will be painful during movement; therefore the teacher will take this into consideration during class participation. In addition to a program of treatment and care, these children will benefit from periods of reduced tensions and rest.

Osteomyelitis

Children with osteomyelitis (inflammation of the bone marrow) will require a program of relative physical inactivity for some time. Only a few years ago this condition was accompanied by many days of draining pus from sinuses or by isolation as maggots were used to remove the diseased area. Today, though, with the use of a variety of well-known antibiotics and other drugs, children need not spend time in the hospital and limbs need not be amputated. School authorities should strive to help prevent further injury to vulnerable areas.

Fracture

The most common condition due to trauma is probably the fracture. Usually the fractures are subdivided into two groups— simple and compound. In the simple fracture there is generally no external wound, and in the compound there is an external wound leading to the site of the break or the bone may be splintered (comminuted). Most children having fractures are permitted to follow fairly normal schedules in the classroom as soon as the initial medical treatment is provided. The plaster casts are cumbersome but they must be utilized and the child must realize that he must wear one until the physician prescribes that it be removed. In most cases, unless it involves the writing hand, the child does not miss much work that the other children are doing at that particular time.

Erb's Palsy

In this condition there is a paralysis of the muscles of the shoulder, arm, and hand. Generally, the arm hangs limp, the hand rotates inward, and normal movements of the arm and hand are usually lost. One of the most common causes of this condition is nerve damage during breech birth. The children having this condition attend regular classes and often try to conceal that anything is wrong with the arm and hand. They do not realize that through disuse the potential functioning ability of the arm and hand may be partially destroyed. Teachers should encourage these children to use the affected limbs.

Bone Imperfections

Teachers will encounter certain children in the regular class-room who have congenital conditions which require special attention. Some children have bones which fracture easily (osteogenesis imperfecta and fragilitas ossium). These children are susceptible to fractures without much cause. A child who jumps from his seat when the bell rings may fracture a bone. Whenever possible these children participate in regular school activities, but the teacher must be on the lookout for possible dangers and steer the child away from them without undue strain.

Wry Neck

This condition is due to a contracture of neck muscles which draws the head to the side of the chin which points in the opposite direction. A teacher may notice that the child is having trouble with his neck and pass the information on to the child's parents. Muscle reeducation and corrective posture are two of the early treatments. The teacher may be asked to help maintain these treatments. A physician should tell the parents what kinds of activities the child must avoid. The parents can pass this information along to the teacher. To neglect this condition may lead to serious curvature of the spine, facial distortion, poor ocular alignment, or body imbalance.

REFERENCES

Brenda, C. E.: *Developmental Disorders of Mentation and Cerebral Palsied.* New York, Grune & Stratton, 1952.

Cardwell, V. E.: *Cerebral Palsy, Advances in Understanding and Care.* New York, North River Press, 1956.

Crothers, B., and Paine, R. S.: *The Natural History of Cerebral Palsy.* Cambridge, Harvard University Press, 1959.

Cruickshank, W. M., and Johnson, G. O.: *Education of Exceptional Children and Youth.* Englewood Cliffs, N. J., Prentice-Hall, 1958.

Denhoff, E.: Cerebral palsy medical aspects. In Cruickshank, W. M., and Raus, G. M. (Eds.): *Cerebral Palsy—Its Individual and Community Problems.* Syracuse, Syracuse University Press, 1955.

Denhoff, E., and Robinault, I.: *Cerebral Palsy and Related Disorders.* New York, McGraw-Hill, 1960.

Dunton, W. R., Jr., and Licht, S. (Eds.): *Occupational Therapy, Principles and Practice.* Springfield, Thomas, 1957.

Guyton, A. C.: *Textbook of Medical Physiology.* Philadelphia, W. B. Saunders, 1956.

Holden, R. H.: A review of psychological studies in cerebral palsy: 1947 to 1952. *American Journal of Mental Deficiency,* 57, 1952.

Hollingworth, L. S.: *Special Talents and Defects.* New York, Macmillan, 1952.

Illingworth, R. S.: The classification, incidence, and causation. In Illingworth, R. S. (Ed.): *Recent Advances in Cerebral Palsy.* Boston, Little, Brown and Co., 1958.

Kirk, S. A., and Weiner, B. B.: *Behavioral Research on Exceptional Children.* Boston, Houghton Mifflin, 1963.

Letourneau, C. U.: The physical therapist. *The Crippled Child,* 1955. Reprint.

Mecham, J.: *Communication Training In Childhood Brain Damage.* Springfield, Thomas, 1966.

The National Foundation for the March of Dimes: *Facts and Figures, 1969.* New York, 1969.

Perlstein, M. A.: Infantile cerebral palsy, classification and correlation. *Journal of American Medical Association, 149,* 1952.

Phelps, W. M.: The cerebral palsied. In Nelson, W. E. (Ed.): *Mitchell Nelson Textbook of Pediatrics.* Philadelphia, W. B. Saunders, 1950.

Rutherford, Berneice R.: *Give Them A Chance to Talk.* Minneapolis, Burgess, 1950.

Tizard, J. P. M.: Cerebral palsy. In Gaisford and Lightwood (Eds.): *Pediatrics.* London, Butterworth, 1955.

Van Riper, C.: *Speech Correction.* New York, Prentice-Hall, 1954.

Willard, H. S., and Spackman, C. S. (Eds.): *Principles of Occupational Therapy.* Philadelphia, J. P. Lippincott, 1957.

Wolfe, W. G., and Reid, L. L.: *A Survey of Cerebral Palsy in Texas.* Austin, United Cerebral Palsy of Texas, 1958.

Chapter 8

THE SOCIALLY AND EMOTIONALLY
MALADJUSTED CHILD IN THE
REGULAR CLASSROOM

T HERE IS CONSIDERABLE overlap between social and emotional maladjustment, although they are not necessarily synonymous. When the child presents sufficiently severe problems that some responsible adult, whether parent or teacher, takes action to do something about him, he becomes the socially or emotionally disturbed child (Mackie, Kvaraceus, and Williams, 1957). Delinquents and psychopaths would be considered socially maladjusted, while the neurotic and psychotic would be emotionally maladjusted.

Today there is an increased awareness of the problems of early discovery and prevention of the socially and emotionally maladjusted. More is being done about community provisions for these children, for that is where the children are when their personal and social difficulties first develop (Mackie, Kvaraceus, and Williams, 1957). In the past fifteen years there has been a marked increase in enrollment in residential school programs for the socially and emotionally maladjusted (Hunter, 1965).

Some emotionally disturbed children may also be considered socially maladjusted. On the other hand, a socially maladjusted child may behave in such a fashion that he is considered emotionally disturbed. The dynamics of behavior in social maladjustment, emotional maladjustment, and delinquency may be the same; therefore the differentiation is a difficult one to make.

SOME DISTINGUISHING CHARACTERISTICS

The outstanding characteristic of the socially maladjusted child is his marked lack of moral development, with an inability to follow approved social behavior. He usually maintains no loyalty to a person or group, profits little from experience, and is frequently in trouble. This person usually has an inadequate conscience and many times deceives others with glib verbalization about standards of morality.

The socially maladjusted child is often referred to as one possessing an antisocial personality. It is true that he often has defective social relationships and cannot make close friends. Because he rejects authority and discipline, it is difficult for him to relate to adults.

The following statements reflect some of the attempts to describe the emotionally maladjusted child. The practical definition given by McCandless (1956) describes the emotionally disturbed child in terms of action:

> A child is emotionally disturbed to a degree that he concerns some responsible person or persons (parents, school administrators, social workers, law enforcement workers) sufficiently that a form of official action is taken about him.

Doll (1952), several years ago, gave a simplified definition of such a child:

> The emotionally disturbed child is most simply interpreted as one who is confused or bewildered. He does not understand his own social stresses, and he feels unaccepted in his efforts to resolve them.

Haring (1963) attempts to be more specific in a recent description:

> The emotionally disturbed child is one who, because of organic and/or environmental influences, chronically displays: (a) inability to learn at a rate commensurate with his intellectual, sensory-motor and physical development; (b) inability to establish and maintain adequate social relationships; (c) inability to respond appropriately in day-to-day life situations; and (d) a variety of excessive behavior ranging from hyperactive, impulsive responses to depression and withdrawal.

This writer, when referring to an emotionally disturbed child, is speaking of a child who has emotional problems that are serious enough to adversely affect his relationship to some aspect of his environment. This includes his self-concept and his interaction with his family, peers, school situation, and/or community life.

Types of Emotional Maladjustment

The emotionally maladjusted child is many times referred to as psychoneurotic and on occasion as psychotic. The neurotic cannot use defense mechanisms properly and in the face of severe stress, resorts to unhealthy neurotic mechanisms. He frequently has a low stress tolerance and becomes anxious and fearful when confronted with conflict and frustration. He is often tense, irritable, and unhappy, and, because they cannot be resolved through healthy mechanisms, these conditions lead to psychological and somatic problems.

In psychotic disorders, the child displays a severe personality decompensation, usually with a marked distortion of reality, and often with loss of contact with reality. Psychotic disorders are divided into two categories—functional and organic—because they may arise from psychological or organic causes or a combination of the two. The functional psychoses are divided into four types: (1) schizophrenic reactions, (2) paranoid reactions, (3) affective psychotic reactions, and (4) involutional psychotic reactions.

The schizophrenic retreats from reality and there is usually a disintegration of the personality. Delusions and hallucinations are common. In paranoid reactions the child maintains an intact personality but has delusions of grandeur or persecution or both. The child suffering from affective reactions has disturbances of mood. He has severe fluctuations in mood, ranging from extreme elation to severe depression. He may also display disturbances of thought patterns along with depression. Involutional psychotic reactions occur generally in later life and would not pertain to the child. The involutional period is usually considered to be from 40 to 65 years.

Defense Mechanisms

The defense mechanisms are learned to protect and enhance the organism. They are called into play when we find ourselves in a position which threatens the ego. These mechanisms help us to soften disappointment, alleviate anxiety, protect ourselves against trauma, and to maintain our feelings of worth and adequacy.

We must consider them normal reactions unless they are carried to an extreme. They can have certain drawbacks, with self-deception and distortion of reality being the two chief ones. They operate on a relatively unconscious level and are not subject to normal checks. As a matter of fact, people resent being told that they are using a defense mechanism.

The following are among the more common defense mechanisms:

escapism	reaction formation
fantasy	undoing
rationalization	regression
projection	identification
repression	introjection
compensation	displacement
emotional insulation	isolation
sublimation	

Coleman (1962) prepared the "Summary Chart of Ego Defense Mechanisms" which follows:

Denial of reality	Protecting self from unpleasant reality by refusal to perceive or face it, often by escapist activities like getting "sick" or being preoccupied with other things.
Fantasy	Gratifying frustrated desires in imaginary achievements.
Rationalization	Attempting to prove that one's behavior is "rational" and justifiable and thus worthy of self and social approval.
Projection	Placing blame for difficulties upon others or attributing one's own unethical desires to others.
Repression	Preventing painful or dangerous thoughts from entering consciousness.
Reaction formation	Preventing dangerous desires from being expressed by exaggerating opposed attitudes and types of behavior and using them as "barriers."
Undoing	Atoning for and thus counteracting immoral desires or acts.

Regression	Retreating to earlier developmental level involving less mature responses and usually a lower level of aspiration.
Identification	Increasing feelings of worth by identifying self with person or institution of illustrious standing.
Introjection	Incorporating external values and standards into ego structure so individual is not at his mercy as external threats.
Compensation	Covering up weakness by emphasizing desirable trait or making up for frustration in one area by over-gratification in another.
Displacement	Discharging pent-up feelings, usually of hostility, on objects less dangerous than those which initially aroused the emotions.
Emotional insulation	Reducing ego involvement and withdrawing into passivity to protect self from hurt.
Intellectualization	Cutting off affective charge from hurtful situations or separating incompatible attitudes by logic-tight compartments.
Sublimation	Gratifying or working off frustrated sexual desires in nonsexual activities.
Sympathism	Striving to gain sympathy from others thus bolstering feelings of self-worth despite failures.
Acting-out	Reducing the anxiety aroused by forbidden desires by permitting their expression.

Prevalence

Today more than half the hospitals beds are occupied by mental patients. Many authorities suggest that at least 10 percent of our school-age population need psychiatric help. Many severely disturbed youngsters are excluded from school each year by expulsion according to the League for Emotionally Disturbed Children. Of the half million children excluded from the schools every year, one in 2,000 needs full-time intensive treatment. In a study conducted in California, Bower (1961) found that 10 percent of the children need either supportive service or intensive special education. Most of the disturbed children in the United States are in the regular classroom, disrupting the school, and retreating further and further from normal social relationships.

The Parent-Child Relationship

Parents of the emotionally disturbed child occupy a unique position among parents of exceptional children. The child who is retarded, blind, deaf, or physically handicapped is usually not so handicapped as the result of any interaction with the parents. However, society often holds the parents of an emotionally disturbed child partially or totally responsible for the child's condition (Ross, 1964).

The findings reviewed in this chapter were gathered by a number of different methods, some more reliable than others. One study, discussed later in the chapter, used clinicians and attempted to analyze the parent-child interaction in order to understand the etiological factors involved in the development of maladjusted behavior in children. The interview and psychological testing of parents were the primary methods used. Usually mothers are tested, either through an interview or a test, and this practice may result in little more than "self-descriptions by extremely ego-involved reporters" (Yarrow, 1963). Psychological tests have not yet demonstrated significant, consistent, and reliable relationships between test scores of the parents and the incidence of problems in their children. Expense and lack of quantifiable measurement tools prevent most clinicians from using the home visit as a source of information. Just recently, clinics have begun using parent-child interaction in a playroom situation as an instrument of measurement, and this action, which is observed, may prove to be quite valid (Schulman, 1967).

The fact that clinicians probe the parent-child relationship in attempting to solve the child's problem implies that there is a significant interaction between parents and their children. Many writers maintain that the personalities of the parents cause the child's difficulties, while others imply that the child's inherent personality traits cause the parents to react to him in unacceptable ways (Klebanoff, 1962). Parents are not generally seen in clinics until their children are obviously quite disturbed. The evaluation of their behavior comes at a time when the child has already been diagnosed as sick. Living with a disturbed child over a long period of time can easily affect parental attitudes and behavior. Ross (1964) states that the child's physiology and the parent's psychology are closely interrelated to the point where an isolation of causal factors is almost impossible.

Many studies support the view that direct causes of emotional disturbance cannot be determined. Kallman and Roth (1956) found that 71.4 percent of the homes of all siblings and dizygotic co-twins and 82 percent of the homes of co-twins and siblings diagnosed as schizophrenic were inadequate. Adequate homes were described as those which (1) were fair or good from a socioeconomic standpoint, (2) had two parents living in the home, and (3) were maintained by parents who were well-adjusted. It is interesting to note, though, that of all the normal co-twins and siblings, nearly two-thirds (64.8%) came from inadequate homes.

Peterson and his associates (1967) found certain general statistical tendencies in their studies, but noted the following:

> We still found families in which the parents appeared maladjusted, evidently didn't get along, and exhibited the most abhorrent kinds of attitudes toward their children, but the children appeared to be getting along beautifully. We saw parents whose attitudes and other characteristics were in nearly perfect congruence with the stereotype of the "good parent," but whose children displayed problems of the most severe order.

The above writers conclude that if all the social influences could be taken into account and measured perfectly, a sizable share of the variance in child behavior would still be unexplained (Peterson *et al.*, 1967).

The literature reveals that many clinicians have drawn conclusions from their instruments of measurement. These people have offered a number of theories to the child, and comprehensive interaction theories that involve the entire family.

Children with emotional problems ranging from night phobia to schizophrenia have parents who appear to have a variety of traits and problems. Mothers of emotionally maladjusted children are typically dominant (McCandless, 1956; Peterson *et al.*, 1967) and overprotective (McCandless, 1956; Klebanoff, 1962; Eisenberg, 1962). On a five-factor scale ranging from suppression to harsh, punitive control (McCandless, 1956), mothers of schizophrenic children appear to be not too warm and close to their children and are less likely to recognize the individuality of the child. They are overpossessive and generally see themselves as sacrificing, suffering women. Often they try to control their children by keeping them dependent and immature. This overprotection may result from taking care of disordered children, or it may be an attempt to deny guilt and conflict over having such children (Shaefer and Bell, 1955).

Specific attitudes can be glimpsed from a list of statements that were endorsed significantly more often by mothers of schizophrenic young men than by mothers of normal young men. The original item numbers are used:

18. A mother should make it her business to know everything her children are thinking.
20. If children are quiet for a little while, a mother should immediately find out what they are thinking about.
32. Children should not annoy parents with their unimportant problems.
33. A devoted mother has no time for social life.
35. A watchful mother can keep her child out of all accidents.
40. Playing too much with a child will spoil him.
22. A son is usually like the mother and a daughter like the father.
23. Punishing a child is a father's job.
61. Parents ought to close their eyes to their children's faults.
62. One reason that it's sad to see children grow up is because they need you more when they are babies.
118. A good mother should shelter her children from life's little difficulties.
123. A child should never keep a secret from his parents.

Mark (1953) developed the test and concludes that mothers of schizophrenic young men are restrictive in control and show attitudes both of cool detachment and of excessive devotion.

Mothers and fathers of problem children in general appear "less well adjusted and sociable, more autocratic, and experience more disciplinary contention" than the parents of more normal children (Peterson, 1967). Kanner (1949) reports that the parents of fifty-five autistic children appear "sophisticated." They have a high level of intelligence but are not comfortable with people, and they have cold and formal married lives. The mothers have little genuine warmth and carry out rules and regulations mechanically. Fathers hardly know their autistic children, are perfectionistic with them, and regard them as interesting objects rather than as human beings. This trait of being unsociable is amplified in more specific terms in at least two studies. These studies show that emotionally disturbed children are more likely to come from homes which are different in some way from other homes in the area (Gerard and Siegel, 1950; Bower, 1962).

One study goes so far as to conclude that the mother is responsible for specific traits in the child, and the father for others:

> Personality problems (sensitivity, absentmindedness, seclusiveness, day-dreaming, inefficiency at work, inferiority feelings, changeability of mood, and nervousness) . . . are related to dictatorial attitudes and a lack of genuine concern among fathers. Conduct problems (truancy from school, truancy from home, stealing, fighting, lying, destructiveness, swearing, disobedience, rudeness, selfishness, and temper tantrums) . . . are related chiefly to maladjustment among mothers and to democratic attitudes and feelings of parental concern among fathers (Peterson, 1967).

The democratic qualities in fathers are usually combined with "laxity, unwillingness to issue orders, exaggerated concern for children and a tendency to shelter them in the face of day-to-day problems" (Peterson, 1967).

Eisenberg (1957) reports that 85 out of 100 fathers of autistic children demonstrated the following traits: "Perfectionistic, detached and humorless, intellectual, preoccupied, ineffective as fathers and husbands." On the other hand, parents of exceptional children are a generally and unusually well informed group regarding medical, psychological, and educational problems pertaining to their children (Cruickshank and Johnson, 1958).

When parents of a disturbed child turn to others for help, what do they find? Since our understanding of the needs of the emotionally maladjusted child is not fully developed, as compared to our understanding of the conditions of other types of exceptional children, parents do not find resources available for helping their emotionally disturbed child. Of course, they do hear opinions, some of which are summarized in the following list:

1. The child is just exaggerating his complaints or feelings, give him a few swats and send him on his way.

2. The child was "born that way" and will never be any different, no matter what you do for him. Don't waste your time, therefore, trying all kinds of efforts to help him; just admit he is a lost cause and go on from there.

3. If he won't adjust to home and family life, then put him in an institution. They know better how to care for such children, and they will make him behave better than you can.

4. Severe emotional disorder is due to a poorly understood hereditary condition. Perhaps drugs will help, but little can be done in the child's environment that will help him.

5. The child has been rejected, repudiated, and unwanted from birth or shortly after, and feels this and is understandably resentful and withdrawn as a result.

6. The child is just going through a phase in development, he will "grow out of it" if you will just give him some time (Haring and Phillips, 1962).

Even with the greatest desire to aid the emotionally disturbed child, the parents may run into very difficult problems. One thing that is extremely important to think about is the effect on the other children in the family. What about their own anger and hostility and feeling of deprivation when they are unable to bring their friends home or live normally in their own home? What about the parents' feelings of guilt? The characteristics of the emotionally maladjusted often makes parents resentful, angry, hurt, and guilty because they are unable to feel for this child the affection they have for others. All these factors have to be considered by all the people concerned.

The disturbances of parental attitudes are more related to the parents' personality than to the totality of role relations within the family group. Just as there is no "typical" family, so is no family with an emotionally disturbed child like any other.

Many instances of deviate behavior are acts that are condoned by people living in lower-class surroundings. Although such behavior is condoned by their parents and peers, children in lower-class surroundings are usually caught by societal agencies and punished for these and other misdemeanors.

Several studies indicate that the behavior displayed by children from lower-class homes is related to the way in which they are treated at home. Mass contrasted the behavior of lower-class and middle-class children and found that lower-class children showed more tendencies toward both submissive behavior and bullying. The behavior expressed by these children reflected the relationships between the children and their parents. Lower-class children also reported more feelings of rejection and unworthiness as a result of family relations than did middle-class children (Lindgren, 1967).

Not only are lower-class children likely to exhibit less emotional control, but many of them learn hostile and destructive patterns of behavior. Many researchers feel that the higher level of emotional disturbances found in lower-class children is due to lack of attention at home. Lower-class families are generally larger than middle-class families, and these parents are unable to devote much individualized attention at home.

In one review of twenty years of research regarding the relationship between social class and maternal behavior, it was found that there exists no difference between lower-class and middle-class mothers in the amount of affection they show toward their children. However, lower-class mothers are much more likely to use severe physical punishment.

Other studies have shown a relation between the severity of attitudes (authoritarian and hostile) and the education of the parent. The direction of such correlation has indicated that the less educated the parents tend to be, the more severe they are with their childen.

EDUCATION

Special Classes

Very few experimental programs have tested the effectiveness of special education for disturbed children. Two researchers in 1959 found special classes with a highly structured approach to be superior to regular school. Although the study did project every indication of success of special education for emotionally disturbed children, it had a small sampling and a brief duration. So far, too, we have only had short-term follow-ups of the children enrolled in special education classes. In order to get the full picture, we must have a long-range follow-up program to provide needed information for evaluating the effectiveness of educational programs for the emotionally maladjusted. Such an evaluation is extremely difficult to make, but parents and educators should not be discouraged—even though debate continues to rage over the idea that psychotherapy of any sort is effective with children.

Regular Classes

It would appear that the emotionally disturbed and socially maladjusted children are provided for in the regular classroom less than other handicapped children. As part of a survey made by the research department of the National Education Association (1967), respondents were asked to indicate whether programs were available for handicapped children through the public school system. Eight out of every ten systems enrolling three hundred or more pupils indicated that they made some provision for mentally retarded children (IQ below 70). Nearly seven in ten of these systems provided for children with severe speech impairments. Slightly more than five in ten reported provisions for children having some degree of hearing loss and for those exhibiting crippling or other special health problems. Forty-six percent provided for visually impaired children. Least frequent (42%) were provisions for emotionally disturbed and socially maladjusted children (Table 8-I).

Educational Engineering

Concerning models in the local public schools for educational programs for emotionally disturbed children, Hewett (1970) has this to say:

> There is the psychotherapeutic model with a psychodynamic, interpersonal emphasis; the pathological or medical model, which focuses on brain pathology and treatment of measured or inferred organic causal factors; and the pedagogical model, concerned with

TABLE 8-I

PROVISIONS OF PROGRAMS FOR HANDICAPPED CHILDREN, 1966

Type of Handicap and Enrollment Group	No Provision Made %	Regular Classes: Specialists Work with Children Individually or in Groups %	All Instruction in Special Classes %	Children Taught at Home by Special Teacher %
Mental retardation (IQ below 70)				
Elementary	22.5	18.2	45.5	1.2
Secondary	47.5	11.4	29.7	0.5
Severe speech impairment				
Elementary	33.2	46.4	11.9	0.8
Secondary	52.8	33.2	7.0	0.5
Deafness or hearing defect				
Elementary	51.2	17.7	8.2	0.9
Secondary	61.9	13.4	4.3	0.6
Crippling and other health problems				
Elementary	51.0	9.5	7.3	15.5
Secondary	61.5	9.4	4.1	12.5
Visual impairment				
Elementary	55.4	17.4	6.3	1.3
Secondary	65.0	13.9	3.3	0.6
Emotional disturbance or social maladjustment				
Elementary	60.2	12.5	11.7	4.3
Secondary	70.7	9.5	6.1	2.8

intellectual development, remedial techniques, and academic goals. Each model has influenced school programs for emotionally disturbed children, and depending on the intuitive, diagnostic, and curriculum skill of the teacher, has been useful to some degree.

Hewett (1970) describes a model called behavior modification which has been useful with emotionally disturbed children. This approach concentrates on bringing the overt behavior of the child into lines required for standards of learning.

Such standards may include development of an adequate attention span; orderly response in the classroom; the ability to follow directions; tolerance for limits of time, space, and activity; approval and avoidance of disapproval.

In Hewett's article, he states that according to Ullman and Krasner (1965) the behavior modifier has three main concerns: (1) defining maladaptive behavior, (2) determining the environmental events which support this behavior, and (3) manipulating the environment in order to alter maladaptive behavior.

The Engineered Classroom

In this type of classroom, Hewett (1970) tells us that the teacher is assigned the role of a behavioral engineer. In this role she attempts to define appropriate task assignments for students and to provide meaningful rewards for learning. She maintains well-defined limits in order to reduce and hopefully to eliminate the occurrence of maladaptive behavior.

The engineered classroom which was investigated by Hewett (1966) was introduced in the public schools by a teacher who had no previous experience with behavior modification theory. She attempted a transfer of this theory not rigidly but pragmatically to the school setting. The teacher organized the behavior modification principle in terms of a learning triangle. The sides of the triangle represent the three essential ingredients for effective teaching. These ingredients are (1) the selection of a suitable educational task for the child, (2) provision of a meaningful reward following accomplishment of that task, and (3) maintenance of a degree of structure under the control of the teacher.

Hewett (1970) comments on the students:

> Two types of students have been enrolled in experimental engineered classrooms to date: public school children with essentially normal intelligence from Santa Monica and Tulare in California and the Palolo School district in Oahu, Hawaii, identified as educationally handicapped (underachieving due to emotional, neurological, or learning disability factors) and emotionally disturbed children hospitalized on the Children's Service of the UCLA Neuro-psychiatric Institute and enrolled in the Neuro-psychiatric Institute School. The public school population consisted mostly of boys with conduct disturbances, neurotic traits including long standing school phobias, psychosomatic and borderline psychotic problems, as well as minimal neurological impairment. The hospitalized group represented more serious emotional problems and included grossly psychotic and more markedly neurologically impaired individuals. All students were in the age group from 8 to 12 (p. 286).

At the time of Hewett's investigation of engineered classroom design, it had been observed in four public school systems for two years; and despite the requirements for teacher aides it appeared to be a feasible design for the public school setting. At that time, Hewett (1970) had this to say about the design:

> The engineered class design is not viewed as an end in itself. Observations suggest that the value of checkmarks and tangible exchange items soon gives way to the satisfaction of succeeding in school and receiving recognition as a student from peers, teachers, and parents. Transition programs have been worked out where children started in the engineered classroom have gradually been reintroduced into regular classes. While this stage is not wholly developed, it appears to be a natural evolutionary development in the program (pp. 291-92).

The treatment of fear or anxiety within an engineered classroom indicates that desensitization is a behavior modfiication technique used with considerable success (Lazarus and Abramovitz, 1962; Bandura, 1969; Patterson, 1965). Systematic application of desensitization traditionally has been restricted to a clinical setting. Kratevz and Forness (1971) report the results of the work they did with a first-grade boy who would not talk while in the classroom. Medical investigation revealed no hearing problem and the origin of the elective mutism was unknown. Achievement testing indicated that the boy was working at grade placement in most subjects.

This child's only means of communication while in the classroom was tugging at the teacher's sleeve or occasionally whispering in her ear. The authors (Kratevz and Forness, 1971) placed the boy in an engineered classroom (Hewett, 1968). The child worked on individual assignments and received checkmarks for working and following behavioral rules of the classroom. The checkmarks were exchanged for candy or small toys at the end of the day.

For this child twelve sessions—two per week—were devoted to the desensitization treatment. According to the authors (Kravetz and Forness) the investigator began by asking the child about favorite heroes and also talking about folk heroes. The young boy at first was reluctant to talk but the investigator verbally reinforced the child's expressed interest in Paul Bunyan.

This type of hero talk was maintained as supportive treatment throughout the rest of the treatment period. The investigator arrived at a hierarchy of fearful situations (Kravetz and Forness, 1971, p. 390):

1. Reading alone to investigator.
2. Reading alone to roommate.
3. Reading to two classroom aides (repeated).
4. Reading to teacher and classroom aides (repeated).
5. Reading to teacher, classroom aides, and small group of classroom peers (repeated).
6. Reading to entire class.
7. Asking question or making comment at weekly ward meeting when all patients, teachers, and staff were present.

Each time the young boy had trouble with any of the sessions the emotive image of Paul Bunyan was introduced into the imaginary situation to overcome unassertive response tendencies. Six weeks after the study was begun the boy was able to raise his hand and make audible comments on two separate occasions.

When the article was written (Kravetz and Fortness, 1971), the boy had been discharged from the hospital and was reportedly functioning well in a regular public school classroom. It should be pointed out that reinforcement techniques, when used alone, did little to resolve the fear the boy had of speaking. Combined use of desensitization and reinforcement as outlined by Bandura (1969) was used and according to the authors (Kravetz and Fortness, 1971) appeared to be necessary for maximum generalization to natural settings. It is also pointed out that another important aspect of the treatment centered around classroom routine. By studying events in the life of Paul Bunyan and drawing pictures of him as academic tasks which were similar to those found in classrooms served as a focal point of a unit of academic instruction. Paul Bunyan's image provoked characteristics such as *strong, big,* and *unafraid.* This seemed to help the boy a great deal.

This study (Kravetz and Fortness, 1971) indicated to this writer that desensitization could also be done in a resource-type room in the regular classroom building. An emotionally disturbed child could go to the resource room periodically for reinforcement and desensitization and then go back to the regular classroom for academic work and socialization with other children.

Other Research

One of the strong considerations of school administrators is whether the cost of special classes for the emotionally disturbed child should be the responsibility of the school. School administrators state that special classes for the emotionally disturbed child are very expensive. This is true, and when people can see only a little improvement in the children, they tend to become discouraged.

Educators have maintained that if they are going to be responsible for the education of these children, then the children must make substantial educational and behavioral gains. This probably is not a valid assumption because many other children in the regular classroom do not make substantial educational and behavioral gains. We are still obligated in America to educate every child to the maximum of his ability.

An experiment was conducted in nine elementary schools in the Arlington, Virginia, county public schools (Haring and Phillips, 1962). The children were moderately to severely emotionally disturbed and had a wide range of behavior symptoms. These children had been receiving service from fifteen highly paid professionals and had shown little improvement. The Arlington County public schools assumed the obligations of developing methods to cope with the behavior of these children and also an educational program for them. Several children were placed in the regular classrooms in six elementary schools in the county. The teachers used methods of teaching generally employed in a regular class setting. They had the help of such professionals as a psychologist, school physician, nurse, elementary supervisor, and remedial reading teacher. These individuals were utilized on a consultative basis. At the end of one year, the children in this group showed an academic achievement gain of one year, which according to Haring and Phillips (1962) is a reasonably good gain considering the lack of modifications and individual attention available in the regular classroom.

Research (Kravetz and Forness, 1971; Hewett, 1968; Bandura, 1969; Patterson, 1965; Haring and Philips, 1962) indicates that the emotionally disturbed child can be educated adequately in a special class or a regular class. Many variables influence the education of these children and the word *adequate* has relative meanings. The fact remains, however, that most emotionally disturbed children are found in the regular classroom; therefore the mildly involved ones can be educated in the regular class with a minimum of additional help for the teacher. The moderately involved ones can be educated in the regular class with the maximum number of consultants needed to help the teacher. The severely involved, emotionally disturbed children should be removed from the regular classroom and should have the help of various therapists to help them get well enough to return to the regular classroom.

REFERENCES

Bandura, A.: *Principles of Behavior Modification.* New York, Holt, Rinehart and Winston, 1969.

Bower, Eli Michael: Comparison of the characteristics of identified emotionally disturbed children with other children in classes. In Trapp, Philip E. and Himelstein, Philip (Eds.): *Readings on the Exceptional Child.* New York, Appleton-Century-Crofts, 1962.

Bower, E. M.: *The Education of Emotionally Handicapped Children.* Sacramento, California State Department of Education, 1961.

Coleman, James C.: *Abnormal Psychology and Modern Life.* Chicago, Scott, Foresman and Co., 1962.

Cruickshank, William, and Johnson, G. Orville: *Education of Exceptional Children and Youth.* Englewood Cliffs, N. J., Prentice-Hall, 1958.

Doll, Edgar A.: Understanding and acceptance. *Exceptional Child, 19,* 1952.

Eisenberg, Leon: School phobia: a study in the communication of anxiety. In Trapp, Philip and Himelstein, Philip (Eds.): *Readings on the Exceptional Child.* New York, Appleton-Century-Crofts, 1962.

Eisenberg, L.: The families of autistic children. *American Journal of Orthopsychiatry, 27,* 1957.

Gerard, D. L., and Siegel, Joseph: The family background of schizophrenia. *Psychiatric Quarterly, 24,* 1950.

Haring, Norris G.: The emotionally disturbed. In Kirk, Samuel A., and Weiner, Bluma B. (Eds.): *Behavioral Research on Exceptional Children.* Washington, Council for Exceptional Children, 1963.

Haring, Norris G., and Phillips, E. Laking: *Educating Emotionally Disturbed Children.* New York, McGraw-Hill, 1962.

Hewett, Frank M.: Educational engineering with emotionally disturbed children. In Jones, Reginald L. (Ed.): *New Directions in Special Education.* Boston, Allyn and Bacon, 1970.

Hewett, F.: *The Emotionally Disturbed Child in the Classroom.* Boston, Allyn and Bacon, 1968.

Hewett, Frank M.: The Tulare experimental class for educationally handicapped children. *California Education, 3,* 1966.

Hunter, Patricia P.: *Education of Handicapped Children in Residential Schools.* U. S. Department of Health, Education and Welfare, 1965.

Kallman, F. J., and Roth, B.: Genetic aspects of preadolescent schizophrenia. *American Journal of Psychiatry, 112,* 1956.

Kanner, L.: Problems of nosology and psychodynamics of early infantile autism. *American Journal of Orthopsychiatry, 19,* 1949.

Klebanoff, Lewis B.: Parental attitudes of mothers of schizophrenia, brain-injured, and retarded, and normal children. In Trapp, Philip E. and Himelstein, Philip (Eds.): *Readings on the Exceptional Child.* New York, Appleton-Century-Crofts, 1962.

Kravetz, Richard J., and Forness, Steven R.: The special classroom as a densensitization setting. *Exceptional Children, 37,* 1971.

Lazarus, A., and Abramovitz, A.: The use of the "emotive imagery" in the treatment of children's phobias. *Journal of Mental Science, 108,* 1962.

Lindgren, Henry Clay: *Educational Psychology in the Classroom.* New York, Wiley, 1967.

McCandless, Boyd R.: The emotionally disturbed child. In Frampton, Merle E. and Gall, Elena D. (Eds.): *Mental and Emotional Deviates and Special Problems. Special Education of the Exceptional.* Boston, Porter, Sargent, 1965, vol. III.

Mackie, Romaine P.; Kvaraceus, William C., and Williams, Harold M.: *Teachers of Children Who Are Socially and Emotionally Maladjusted.* U. S. Office of Education, 1957.

Mark, J. C.: The attitudes of the mothers of male schizophrenics toward child behavior. *Journal of Abnormal Social Psychology, 48,* 1953.

National Education Association, Washington Research Division: *NEA Research Bulletin, 45* (No. 4), 1967.

Patterson, G.: A learning theory approach to the treatment of the school phobic child. In Ullman, L. and Krasner, L. (Eds.): *Case Studies in Behavior Modification.* New York, Holt, Rinehart and Winston, 1965.

Peterson, Donald, *et al.*: Parental attitudes and child adjustment. In Medinnus, Gene R. (Ed.): *Readings in the Psychology of Parent-Child Relations.* New York, Wiley, 1967.

Ross, Alan O.: *The Exceptional Child in the Family.* New York, Grune & Stratton, 1964.

Schulman, Robert E., *et al.*: Laboratory measurement of parental behavior. In Medinnus, Gene R. (Ed.): *Readings in the Psychology of Parent-Child Relations.* New York, Wiley, 1967.

Shaefer, E. S., and Bell, R. A.: *Parental Attitude Research Instrument: Normative Data.* Preliminary working draft from the section on Child Development, Laboratory of Psychology, National Institute of Mental Health, Bethesda, 1955.

Ullman, L., and Krasner, L. (Eds.): *Case Studies in Behavior Modification.* New York, Holt, Rinehart and Winston, 1965.

Yarrow, Marian Radke: Problems of methods in parent-child research. *Child Development, 34,* 1963.

Chapter 9

THE CHILD WITH LEARNING DISABILITIES
IN THE REGULAR CLASSROOM

THE CHILD WITH learning difficulties has been labeled with many names. He seems to have the capacity to learn, but the normal way to learn is harder for him for a multitude of reasons. The child with learning disabilities is classified as being on an achievement level one year or more below the normal capacity for achievement of children his age.

DEFINITION

The United States Office of Education (1968) has adopted the following definition of learning disability:

> Children with special learning disabilities exhibit a disorder in one or more of the basic psychological processes . . . They include conditions which have been referred to as perceptual handicaps, brain injury, minimal brain dysfunction, dyslexia, and developmental aphasia . . . They do *not* include learning problems which are due primarily to visual, hearing, or motor handicaps, to mental retardation . . . (p. 34).

This child with learning disabilities, or, as some refer to the condition, minimal brain dysfunction, usually has near-average, average, or above-average intelligence but has certain disabilities in learning and/or behavior. These disabilities may range from mild to severe and are attributed by many to malfunctions of the central nervous system. These disabilities may appear as different combinations of difficulties in perception, conceptualization, language, memory, and control of attention, impulse, or motor function.

No one has really found the exact cause of learning dis-

172

abilities or minimal brain dysfunction. There are many theories, however. It has been attributed to genetic factors, biochemical imbalance, brain injury or neurological dysfunction, and to serious emotional or social problems.

Who is the child with learning disabilities? Daly (1965) labels him an enigma. He belongs to a category of exceptional children which is easier to describe than to define. This child's exceptionality is called by many names but the two most prominent are special learning disabilities and minimal brain dysfunction. Capobianco (1967) feels a term referring to brain injury fails to serve any practical function. Another authority advocates that there are only two sources of learning disabilities—brain injury and emotional disturbance—each a distinct category not to be included under learning disabilities generally (Siegel, 1968).

Educators feel more comfortable with the term learning disability and medical-clinical people lean toward the scientific label (Koblock, 1966). Regardless of the lack of agreement about definition, the child with learning disabilities is probably best described as one who manifests an educational discrepancy between his mental capacity for learning and his actual level of functioning.

The difficulties of the child with learning disabilities ". . . are attributed to damage to the parts of the brain which regulate the way an individual "sees" things after his senses have presented the facts to him and to damage to the parts which control his movements and his impulses" (Lehman and Hall, 1966, p. 10).

The definition of the National Project on Minimal Brain Dysfunctions in Children reads as follows:

> Minimal brain dysfunction as a diagnostic and descriptive category refers to children of near average, average, or above average intellectual capacity with certain learning and/or behavior disabilities ranging from mild to severe, which are associated with deviations of function of the central nervous system. These deviations may manifest themselves by various combinations of impairment in perception, conceptualization, language, memory, and control of attention, impulse, or motor function.
>
> These aberrations may arise from genetic variations, biochemical

irregularities, perinatal brain insults or other illnesses or injuries sustained during the years critical for the development and maturation of the central nervous system, or from unknown organic causes.

During the school years, a variety of learning disabilities is the most prominent manifestation of the condition which can be designated by this term (Clements, 1966).

The child with learning disabilities with average or above intelligence has baffled parents and educators for years. This child is often referred to by teachers as immature, a slow learner, undisciplined, or emotionally maladjusted. He is usually retarded in one or more of the processes of speech, language, reading, writing, arithmetic, or spelling. Parents have considered him lazy, hard to control, scatter-brained, or just highstrung. Strauss and Lehtinen (1947) made the following statement: "These disturbances prevent or impede a normal learning process."

These perceptionally handicapped children have been pressured by their parents and teachers, and failure has been more the rule than the exception. They are often on the defensive and many feel quite hostile toward their parents and teachers. The behavior of these children make many of them as unacceptable to their peers as to adults.

The behavioral patterns most frequently seen are a short attention span, distractibility, hyperactivity, and impulsiveness (Clements, Lehtinen, and Lukens, 1964). One of the most obvious of the difficulties which are characteristic of the child with learning disabilities is his distractibility, or over-sensitivity to stimuli (Strauss and Kephart, 1955).

The normal child usually inhibits his response to stimulating situations and his overt behavior is not intense. The opposite is usually true of the child with learning difficulties. His activities are very intense, he responds to many stimuli, and expends a great amount of energy. This is an effect of not being able to face up to stress due to weakened adaptive behavior or so called "concept of vulnerability" (Koblock, 1966).

When this child changes from one activity to another, he shows a tendency to be preoccupied with repetition of the former stimuli. This perseveration is another of the obvious characteristics of the brain-injured child, whether minimal or major damage is involved.

DIAGNOSIS

The bizarre behavior and inability of this child to learn in the traditional classroom are usually the forces which instigate parents to take the first steps toward seeking help. The financial status of the parents is a governing factor in determining the procedure. Probably the best, and the least expensive, diagnostic facility available to them would be a public-supported child guidance clinic. Here a team approach is provided. Psychiatrist, psychologist, neurologist, educational consultant, speech therapist, and pediatrician correlate their findings in diagnosis and therapy.

Referral to the clinic is usually made by the teacher or family physician. Before the child is seen, a school report should be obtained from the teacher, social worker, and the guidance counselor. A developmental history must be obtained from the parents, and later the child and the parents are called in for interviews.

Testing

At the child guidance clinic various psychological and educational tests are administered to the child. The complete Wechsler Intelligence Scale for Children, the Bender Visual-Motor Gestalt, and a reading evaluation are necessary for the preliminary evaluation. This is one situation where psychological tests can be quite valuable.

Hanvik (1961 describes some of the psychological diagnostic tools used in a Child Guidance Clinic. They included a test battery consisting of the following: (1) Wechsler Intelligence Scale for Children, (2) Bender Gestalt, (3) Goodenough Draw-A-Man, (4) Seguin Form Board, (5) Knox Cube Test, (6) Porteus Mazes, (7) Memory for Design Test, (8) Raven Progressive Matrices, (9) Cerebral Dominance Test, and (10) Jastak Wide-Range Reading Test. In addition to this battery, the individual child also received a behavior rating scale with ten items involved.

Clinical observations in a study by Temmer (1965) indicated that a subject's level of performance on the Bender-Gestalt designs corresponds roughly with the degree of general intelligence as measured by standard tests, such as the Wechsler. The subjects are divided into two groups: those with known neurological involvement and those for whom no neurological involvement was recorded. Since the better the performance, the fewer the errors, there was an inverse relationship between the Bender-Gestalt and the intelligence quotient .

> In a neurologically damaged individual, the usual "general intelligence" interpretation of the Intelligence Quotient needs to be qualified. If, for instance, manipulative and perceptual functions are selectively impaired, not only the performance, but also the full Intelligence Quotient is lowered, although the person may be capable of performing verbally at a superior level. Similarly, the Bender-Gestalt score, in such a case, is lowered and therefore ceases to reflect "general intelligence" as it does in the case of neurologically intact subjects . . . the overall inferiority of the brain damaged on drawing tasks is found quite consistently (Temmer, 1965, p. 145).

Clements and Peters (1962) thus far have isolated three principal patterns in the Wechsler Intelligence Scale for Children. The most common pattern is "scatter" in either or both the verbal and performance scales (W.I.S.C. Pattern I). Low scores most frequently occur in arithmetic and digit span in the verbal scale and block design, object assembly, coding, and mazes in the performance scale.

The second most frequent pattern (W.I.S.C. Pattern II) is that in which the verbal intelligence quotient is fifteen to forty points higher than the performance intelligence quotient. The third and least frequent pattern (W.I.S.C. Pattern III) is the reverse of the W.I.S.C. Pattern II, i.e. the performance intelligence quotient is fifteen to forty points higher than the verbal intelligence quotient.

While the W.I.S.C. is an important diagnostic tool in measuring perceptual disorders, the Bender Visual-Motor Gestalt is used to measure the perception and the visual-motor coordination of the child with learning disabilities. There are several reading tests which can be used to measure the sight-reading ability and determine reading level, types of errors, and comprehension of material.

The child with learning disabilities can have many kinds of distortions in symbolic perception, expression, and thinking. Kirk and McCarthy (1961) have devised a test of psycholinguistic abilities for children whose ages range between two and nine.

The idea of the test is to determine which functions the child has developed and which ones he has not. For example, a child may be able to see and speak adequately but may not be able to follow directions. There are times when a child understands what he hears but cannot interpret what he sees. The nine subtests of the Illinois Test of Psycholinguistic Abilities attempt to determine abilities and disabilities in children so that remedial instruction can be programmed.

Bateman (1964) points out that assessment of both the level of performance and manner of performance over a period of time are necessary for an accurate picture of test results.

Scherer (1961) made an investigation to identify relevant variables which would significantly contribute to the long-range prediction of academic achievement in brain-injured children. More specifically, its objective was to determine the intellectual, personality, and physical status variables which might predict successful academic achievement in these children. He felt the study was important because the psychologist is continually called upon to make predictions in this area.

There is reason to believe, however, that there are variables other than intellectual, personality, and physical status which are important, about which information is not on hand, and which would be necessary for successful prediction. Among these are (1) information concerning academic readiness programs to which the child will be exposed, either at home or in a school situation, (2) the effect of future diseases and accidents, and (3) the child's future social environment.

Lezak and Dixon (1964) did a case study of ninety-nine children and concluded there is not enough longitudinal data to support much of what has been accepted as adequate diagnostic measures for learning disabilities.

The very fact that we cannot exchange parents or repair damaged brains has led to the present-day concern of many with behavioral and symptomatic rather than pathological or etiological factors in making predictions (Bateman, 1964).

In discussing diagnostic procedures, Clements and Peters (1962) recommend the use of the entire Wechsler Intelligence

Scale for Children. The Bender Visual-Motor Gestalt, Gray's or Gates' reading test, and a small number of appropriate picture cards from the Michigan Picture Test are used for personality assessment. They feel that clues to personality are constantly being produced by the child and observed by the examiner during the work-up; therefore a standardized projective technique, such as drawing persons or objects, long interviews, and the Rorschach are inadequate even as screening devices.

Clements (1963) has compiled a checklist of the discernible features of the child with learning disabilities. Not all symptoms are likely to appear in a given child:

> *Normal or Above General Intelligence* (as determined from either the Verbal or Performance Scale of the WISC) . . . The important consideration here is that results of intelligence evaluation clearly indicate that although achievement is variable depending on the nature of the task, the overall level of intellectual functioning is within normal limits and that we are *not* dealing with a child who is generally mentally retarded, that is, deficient in all areas of endeavor.
>
> *Specific Learning Deficits*—Child cannot read at grade or age level: a mildly stressful situation may bring forth typical dyslexic errors; spelling poor; difficulty with abstractions and whole-part relationships; difficulty in mastering tasks which are dependent upon intact visual-motor-perceptual integration.
>
> *Perceptual-motor Deficits*—Printing, writing, and drawing poor; poor and erratic performance when copying geometric figures (Bender Visual Motor Gestalt Teest); often attempts to compensate for the latter by task-perseverance and/or innumerable and meticulous tiny strokes of the pencil; often has difficulty in reproducing geometric designs with blocks; difficulty with figure-ground and/or whole-part discrimination.
>
> *General Coordination Deficits*—Child often described as awkward or clumsy; this may appear in either fine muscle performance or in overall coordination, or both.
>
> *Hyperkinesis* (or less frequently, hypokinesis)—Child appears to be in constant motion, flitting from one object or activity to another, or may be merely restless and fidgety; we have considered that the child's "driveness" may manifest also as voluble, uninhibited speech, or as disorganized thinking, even in the absence of outward hyperactivity. Some children with learning and behavior symptoms and one or more "equivocal" neurological signs do not show hyperkinesis, but instead can be described as "slow as molasses," since they move, think, and talk at a very reduced rate. Frequently, this

slow responding child will have an "asphasoid" quality in his speech.

Impulsivity—The child cannot keep from touching and handling objects, particularly in a strange or over-stimulating environment; he frequently speaks without checking himself; he may curse, be insulting, or eagerly relate all the family secrets. His impulsivity easily leads him into conflict with the demands of conformity as established by family, school, and society. Some children may commit striking anti-social acts, to the point of fire setting, stealing, and even murder, with only a medium of provocation.

Emotional Liability—The child may be "highstrung," irritable, aggressive, or easily moved to tears; he will have quick changes of emotional behavior from high temper to easy manageability and remorse; he may be panicked by what would appear to others as a minimally stressful situation; however, some are again at the opposite end of the continuum in that they are consistently sweet-and-even tempered, cooperative, diligent, and display a very high frustration tolerance.

Short Attention Span and/or Distractibility—The child is unable to concentrate on one thing for very long; he especially fades out when abstract material is being presented. Even with this symptom, some show a tendency to become locked in a simple repetitious motor activity or preoccupation with one verbal topic. Some children show fair attention span when their interest is aroused, but when not so engaged, display marked distractibility to casual stimuli.

"Equivocal" or "Soft" Neurological Signs—Among the most frequently seen of such signs are: transient strabismus; dysdiadochokinesis; poor coordination of fingers; mixed and/or confused laterality; speech defect, or a history of slow speech development or irregularity; and general awkwardness.

Borderline Abnormal or Abnormal EEG—Although agreement in this area is not complete, the high frequency of borderline or abnormal brain wave test records reported is felt to be significant.

Use of the brain wave as a method of identifying the brain injured is a highly controversial area. Some authorities feel that there is a possible disturbance of function of the diencephalon. The most frequent neurological signs found have been gross coordination irregularities, perceptual-motor difficulties, fine coordination defect, strabismus, reading difficulty, dysdiadochokinesia, mixed laterality, some degree of ambidexterity, and speech defect. Clements and Peters (1962) state that this type of comprehensive and time-consuming diagnostic procedure also includes EEG findings.

Neurologist Cohn (1964) points out that current neurological practice cannot determine with precision the correlation between minimal signs in EEG and learning disabilities.

Hanvik (1961), in a study of children with abnormal EEG's, found a difference on the Bender-Gestalt Test ratings and on coding subtest scores of the Wechsler Intelligence Scale for Children but on no other battery of tests. In children with learning disabilities, Hanvik found medical and neurological findings were not significantly different between the normal EEG group and the abnormal EEG group.

According to research concerning the importance of the EEG, it should be stated that thousands more readings are needed with adequate controls using children who have no problem of hyperactivity, retarded children, hyperactive children, children with emotional problems, and those in other categories. Many of the studies have been useful, provocative, and pioneering but very limited in scope. It would seem then that the opinion of the experts is not unanimous.

TREATMENT

Other differences exist in the opinions of the authorities. Some authorities feel that the child and his family need counseling and psychiatric help and that medication is at best superficial. Clements and Peters (1962) feel that treatment and management can be handled by a combination of drugs and infrequent counseling.

In describing his treatment plan, Clements (1963) feels the medication is a most important adjunct. For the purpose of reducing hyperactivity and irritability, captodiamine hydrochloride (Suvren®), a psychic activator which lengthens attention span, is used. Thioridazine hydrochloride (Mellaril®), which has a specificity of action on certain brain sites as a tranquilizer; and the amphetamines (Dexedrine® and Benzedrine®), which ordinarily stimulate activity but in minimal brain dysfunction have a calming effect, are prescribed (*Physicians' Desk Reference to Pharmaceutical Specialties and Biologicals,* 1961). Since children do not respond to drugs and dosages in the same manner, it is often necessary to experiment with different medications and dosages for a period of time to determine the best and most useful prescription for a particular child. After the drug is regulated, the child is assigned to a "medication management" clinic. These children are seen at two to three month intervals for checkups and blood studies (Clements, 1693).

EDUCATION

In the past, the child with learning disabilities was either ignored or forgotten. The child could not behave like other children and consequently did not learn, so the teacher either thought he was a "bad" child or terribly dumb. She would feel guilty at what she thought were her own failures or become so infuriated at this child that she would lose self-control. He was usually passed from one grade to the next not because he did the work, but because the teacher could not stand to have him in her class another year. Most of these students became so rebellious and frustrated themselves that if they could they would become dropouts.

There have been many theories in the last few years concerning the best way to educate children with learning disabilities. Each theory has good and bad points, and someday the right one will be found—which may prove to be a culmination of all the others.

When learning disabilities were first brought to the awareness of the medical profession, as well as the educational profession, it was decided that the best way to educate these children was to segregate them from the others, so that they could learn at their own pace without the frustrations and pressures of the public school. Therefore, special schools were established. However, this was quite expensive, so the government set up financial assistance to help public and private schools establish special education classes within the schools. This is the way the system was set up during the 1960's. The trend now, however, is to abolish the special education classes and the segregation and move this child with learning disabilities back into the regular classroom.

The needs of all children are the same whether they be

normal or with learning problems. The main goal of the teacher is to teach the child. The teacher must in essence be a therapist, one who is readily aware of each child's needs and be patient, understanding, and kind toward each of her children—those who are easy to manage and those who are difficult. This teacher must be willing to learn every day and to put new ideas, new materials, and new experiences before the child. This person should be aware that the child with learning disabilities cannot always control his emotions, and she must expect many differences in his day-to-day behavior. The teacher must acknowledge that the child with learning disabilities does not intentionally behave in a manner that is frustrating to other people.

The teacher should be watchful of an impending castastrophic situation—that is, one in which the child becomes so frustrated he loses his composure. He may react in one of several ways, such as bursting into tears or screaming and beating the desk. If the teacher is aware that this may happen and knows the symptoms to look for, she can help the child before he completely loses control. At this time, he needs to stop the task he is doing and be consoled. The teacher may remove him to the nurse's station or hall and comfort him, then tell him he can return when he feels better. If she is able to catch the warning signals and help him before he loses control, then she can save him a great amount of embarrassment in front of his classmates.

The Montessori method in some ways is related to, and can be very helpful in, teaching children with learning disabilities. There are several such schools around the country, and although Dr. Montessori's ideas on management in education were established for normal children, there is much common ground between her method and that of teaching children with learning disabilities. In the Montessori method the child is thought of and respected for what he is. The learning procedures are given in sequential order; the teacher's main objective is to watch each child closely and find out what his needs and abilities to function are so that he can progress in his own way. The child goes through the stages of training at his own pace, and the classroom is joyful while working at learning.

The environment in school for the child with learning disabilities should be planned in order to counteract in as many ways as possible the organic problems of hyperactivity and distractibility which he often displays. The curriculum should be geared to the basic skills of reading, writing, spelling, and arithmetic, and should also include activities in the particular perceptual areas of disturbance which are a major source of the child's problems.

Many authorities say that the best school situation for children with perceptual difficulties requires a carefully controlled environment and a teacher trained in this area of special education. However, few such teachers and environments can be found.

Strauss and Kephart (1955) state that simplicity in the physical setting is a must to protect the child from the distractions he is not able as yet to ignore. He reacts best in a very small group where the children sit well apart. Routine and orderly procedures help him to function better. Some of these children may work better away from the other children or even secluded behind a screen. It is hoped that later these children will be able to move back with the other children.

It is believed by some that the child's interest and attention span must control the kind and length of lessons; therefore short, varied lessons with spaced practice would be best. The skills should be presented one at a time with continued review. The use of variety in presentation will help the child to generalize (Clements, Lehtinen, and Lukens, 1964).

It is imperative that the teacher interpret the pattern of weakness and design the learning situation for each child. This points out that global measures are not important to teachers. Specific information on behavior which the teacher is concerned with is required (Sabatino, Wickham, and Burnett, 1968).

The normal child's visual perception is characterized by his ability to recognize at a glance the details of an object and to immediately perceive it as a whole. The whole is also perceived as an object in the foreground against a background. Strauss and Kephart (1955) believe that the child with learning disabilities responds to the details but cannot combine them into the whole. He also has difficulty in perceiving the object in the foreground as he will be distracted by the background.

For the child with poor visual perception, color can be used to heighten certain aspects of the visual stimulus. Verbal description while tracing kinesthetically will help the child to hold attention until the most important features are correctly perceived (Strauss and Kephart, 1955).

Auditory perception problems result in the child's failure to discover the significant relationships between sounds. Edgington and Blackmon (1962) say that color cues are very helpful in reinforcing verbal concepts. It is stated that auditory-visual relationships will be strengthened if the child can hear his own voice; therefore silent reading is not emphasized until the child has overcome many of his academic problems.

Strauss and Lehtinen (1947) state that the brain-injured child sometimes lacks the ability to discover the significant relationships of numbers. He cannot visually perceive number combinations and relate them to other number groups. Drills should not be used as the child will memorize. Insight should be gained through frequent experiences with concrete and semi-concrete materials.

Disturbance in visual perception may also result in the child copying letters rather than writing them from memory. The child should be required to reproduce written forms from memory, and writing should be correlated with reading (Strauss and Lehtinen, 1947).

Realistically, we cannot really appreciate the problem of the perceptually handicapped child because we cannot truly experience it. Nevertheless a thorough knowledge of the problem, the proper methods and procedures, and the day-to-day observation and evaluation of the processes used by the child are important factors in helping these children to overcome their feelings of inadequacy and discouragement (Clements, Lehtinen, and Lukens, 1964).

Many of the children require a special school program planned to meet their individual needs. It has been found, however, that a large percentage of these children remain in the traditional classrooms in the local public schools. Special education classes of this type have not been set up as yet in the public schools in most localities, and only a small percentage of the parents are financially able to send their child to a private school. There are very few schools in existence which specialize in teaching the child with learning disabilities, and these schools are quite expensive and have long waiting lists. The private tutor is utilized by many parents, but to find one with the special qualifications needed is a major task.

Children with learning disabilities are sometimes found in the classes for the educable mentally retarded in the schools which have not set up a special education class for the child with learning disabilities who has a normal IQ. The educational approaches and the educational goals are quite different for the learning-disabled child with normal IQ than for the organically impaired child in the borderline intellectual classification. This must be taken into account, for the outcomes of the failure could very well result in frustration for the teacher and injustice to the child (Clements, Lehtinen, and Lukens, 1964).

Education for children with learning disabilities in the public schools usually occurs in one of two places—the resource room or the self-contained special classroom. Today, if there is any facility available for teaching these children, it should be one of these two.

The self-contained special classroom is usually for the more severely involved individual. If his learning and behavior are so inappropriate that he cannot function in the regular classroom for periods of time, then he is transferred to this self-contained special class. This room usually has from eight to fifteen children depending on the teacher, whether she is experienced and whether she has teacher aides. These children are usually of varying ages and remain in the classroom all day. The teacher teaches to each child's specific needs. Aides are used to help the teacher in many ways. These are women who come in as volunteers from the Parent-Teacher Association, parents, women's civic clubs, or certified aides hired by the school system. The child usually stays in this type of situation from two to six years. Most children with learning disabilities should remain in the regular classroom.

The resource room is for the less severe learning and behavioral problems. These classrooms, too, have a teacher and some aides. The child comes to the resource room for remedial work. This period of time may be from one to three hours per day. The rest of the school day he stays in his regular classroom. Because scheduling the child at the best time may become a problem, there must be very careful planning between the resource teacher, the regular classroom teacher, and the school administrator. This room should never have more than ten children at any one time, but because it is a come-and-go situation, the teacher can serve as many as twenty-five within the school year. The teacher gives individualized instruction or instructs in small groups. Every school should have a resource room.

Some good suggestions for teaching children with learning disabilities have been prepared for the classroom teacher by the Special Education Center at the Louisiana State University in New Orleans (1970). They are as follows:

CHILDREN WITH LEARNING DISABILITIES

Suggestions for the Classroom Teacher

1. Permit the child to use any learning crutch he needs. (E.g. if he needs his fingers to count or point, let him use them.)

2. If the child has problems with numbers and number concepts let him use his fingers.

3. The school or parent must find someone to serve as a "reader" for this child. He will then have his assignments read to him.

4. Oral examinations for test results should be given.

5. Special reading materials of high interest value for his age, yet at his reading level should be used.

6. Remember that his speech, reception, and expression of information is often at a slower rate. It takes him more time to "take in," integrate and "give out" information. Give him that time.

7. Find him a sheltered learning place. A place with less distraction will help him work better.

8. "Cut down" on the amount of work he must do or give him an equal amount of work in several small groups. (E.g. instead of one page containing twenty problems, cut the problems into five strips of four problems each. After he has completed one strip, he will come to you for the next, and the next.)

9. Many of these children have undetected auditory problems. He often is confused by a series of directions. Give one direction at a time, allow time to complete the task before the next is given.

10. Grading is difficult. If the child has a known spelling problem, grade him for his *content* in a book report rather than lowering his grade due to spelling errors. This applies to other subject matter too. He is, unfortunately, all too aware of his reading, spelling, or arithmetic inadequacy—don't remind him.

11. Consistently point out his strong points, give him ready support and encourage all efforts whether successful or not. "Set up" success situations for him as often as you can.

These suggestions can and should become as familiar to the classroom teacher as the methods she uses for teaching other skills to other children.

The suggestion has been made "that we move from defining exceptional children to defining exceptional situations within the school" (Lilly, 1970, p. 48). This seems to be a way to get to the problems in the right perspective, taking some of the blame of the child's failure off him and placing that part of the blame where it possibly deserves to be—that is, within the school.

Teachers and administrators must be educated to this idea of placing the exceptional child in the regular classroom, whether he be a child with learning disabilities or some other exception from the norm. Unless the child is severely involved in his handicap, the thinking of many professionals today is to put that child in the regular classroom in public or private schools.

HOME MANAGEMENT

In a recent article (Clements, 1966, p. 3) the following suggestions were given to help in the home management of children with learning disabilities:

1. A consistent "wake-up" time each morning.
2. Regulated bed-time and nap-time (when appropriate).
3. Meals to be served at the same time each day.
4. The child's regular activities should be on a time-table schedule, i.e. a specific and consistent time for play, watching television, homework and study, chores, etc.

In disciplining the child, above all remember not to punish him for the behavior he cannot control and be consistent in what you demand of him. Always follow the offense with the punishment so that the inappropriate behavior will be recognized by the child. Never continually punish the child. Punish him and forget it. Also, remember to reward and praise him for his accomplishments. The main thing to remember is that the behavior is what is wrong so "punish the behavior not the child" (Clements, 1966, p. 5).

REFERENCES

Bateman, Barbara: Learning disabilities—yesterday, today, tomorrow. *Exceptional Children, 31,* 1964.

Capobianco, R. J.: Diagnostic methods used with learning disability cases. *Exceptional Children, 31,* 1967.

Clements, Samuel D.: Minimal brain dysfunctions in children—terminology and identification. U. S. Public Health Service, Monograph 3, Publication 1415, 1966.

Clements, Samuel D.: The child with minimal brain dysfunction—a profile. *Children with Minimal Brain Injury.* Chicago, National Society for Crippled Children and Adults, 1963.

Clements, Samuel D., and Peters, John E.: Minimal brain dysfunction in the school-age child. *Archives of General Psychiatry, 6,* 1962.

Clements, Samuel D.; Lehtinen, L. E., and Lukens, J. E.: *Children with Minimal Brain Injury.* Chicago, National Society for Crippled Children and Adults, 1964.

Cohn, Robert: The neurological study of children with learning disabilities. *Exceptional Children, 31,* 1964.

Daly, William C.: Minimal brain damage—an enigma. *Catholic Education Review, 63,* 1965.

Edington, Ruth, and Blackmon, Lillian: Helping Children with Reading Disability. Little Rock, Child Guidance Unit, University of Arkansas Medical Center, 1962.

Hanvik, Leo: Diagnosis of cerebral dysfunction in the child. *American Journal of Diseases of Children, 100,* 1961.

Kirk, Samuel A., and McCarthy, James J.: The Illinois test of psycholinguistic abilities—an approach to differential diagnosis. *American Journal of Mental Deficiency, 66,* 1961.

Koblock, Peter: Brain injury and maladjustive behavior in adolescent youth. *High School Journal, 49,* 1966.

Lehman, Eileen F., and Hall, Robert E.: Who is this child? *American Education,* April, 1966.

Lezak, Muriel D., and Dixon, Henry, Jr.: The brain injured children in a clinical population: a statistical description. *Exceptional Children, 30,* 1964.

Lilly, M. S.: Special education: a teapot in a tempest. *Exceptional Children, 37,* 1970.

Physician's Desk Reference to Pharmaceutical Specialties and Biologicals, 16th ed. Oradell, N. J., Medical Economics, Inc., 1961.

Sabatino, David; Wickham, William, and Burnett, C. W.: The Psycho-educational Assessment of Learning Disabilities. *Catholic Educational Review, 66,* 1968.

Scherer, Isidor, W.: The prediction of academic achievement in brain-injured children. *Exceptional Children, 28,* 1961.

Siegel, Ernest: Learning disabilities: substance or shadow. *Exceptional Children, 34,* 1968.

Special Education Center: Children with Learning Disabilities—Suggestions for the Classroom Teacher. Unpublished manuscript, Louisiana State University in New Orleans, 1970.

Strauss, A. A., and Kephart, N. C.: *Psychopathology and Education of the Brain-Injured Child.* New York, Grune & Stratton, 1955, Vol. II.

Strauss, A. A., and Lehtinen, L. E.: *Psychopathology and Education of the Brain-Injured Child.* New York, Grune & Stratton, 1947.

Temmer, Helena W.: Wechsler intelligence scores and Bender-Gestalt performance in adult male mental defectives. *American Journal of Mental Deficiency, 70,* 1965.

U. S. Department of Health, Education, and Welfare, Office of Education: Special education for handicapped children—toward fulfillment of the nation's commitment . . . *First Annual Report.* National Advisory Committee on Handicapped Children, January 31, 1968.

Chapter 10

SPECIAL HEALTH PROBLEMS IN THE REGULAR CLASSROOM

C HILDREN WITH SPECIAL health problems are those whose weakened physical condition renders them relatively inactive or slow, or requires special precautions. Low vitality is a term that was used quite often in previous years to refer to a child with a chronic or special health problems.

These children more often than not have at least normal intelligence and should be treated and taught like normal children. If at all possible, these children with low vitality should be placed in the regular classroom; they must be kept in the mainstream and not segregated. The teacher must look at the child's educational needs just as she should any normal child's in the class. She should not place a cloud or shell around this child, and she has to have faith in the child.

Children with special health problems have a variety of chronic ailments which confine them to bed for relatively long periods of time or curtail their activity periodically or chronically.

PARENTAL ATTITUDES

In the search for information pertaining to parental attitudes toward these children, five reactions of parents were found to be more common than others. These were (1) anxiety, (2) disbelief, (3) hostility, (4) helplessness, and (5) resentment.

A serious threat occurs to the set of values an individual establishes as a parent when a child in the family is sick for a long period of time. The dismay, the fear of the unknown concerning the condition in the child's future, and the feeling of helplessness combine to make the burden great. Often parents cannot bring themselves to face the reality of this type of handicap. They try to keep the neighbors from knowing; they may neglect to seek the help they need; or they may go from one doctor to another refusing to believe the diagnosis. Many times they are really trying to find someone who will tell them that it is not as bad as they fear.

The term "special health problems" encompasses a multiplicity of conditions. Cardiac conditions, spina bifida, malnutrition, epilepsy, diabetes, allergic disorders, anemia, tuberculosis, various crippling conditions, and leukemia are some of them. The common elements in all of these conditions include chronic illness, the need for continuing medical attention, and certain restrictions of activity necessarily imposed on the individual.

Although research has been conducted on specific special health problems, there is little in the literature concerning the general topic of parental attitudes toward children with special health problems. The available material deals with the more general topic of parental attitudes toward handicapped children. Parental attitudes toward all types of handicaps do not seem to be influenced by the causative factors or the severity of the handicap as much as by the general adjustment of the parents. In other words, the better adjusted the parent, the better able he is to cope with the handicap of the child.

When considering parental reactions to a special health problem, it is important to remember that in some instances these health problems develop after the child has lived a normal life for some period of time. Many of these children are normal at birth and their problem develops later. In some cases the condition is apparent or at least suspected during infancy.

DIABETES

For hundreds of years, man has recorded facts and feelings concerning the disease we know as diabetes. Why should the average man know about diabetes? The answer is simple. One of the most common diseases today, diabetes affects about four million persons in the United States, and estimates indicate that another five and one-half million are potential diabetics. More than one and one-half million of the four million are unaware that they have the disease. The possibility of becoming a diabetic increases with age and other known circumstances. Furthermore, medical progress has made it possible to more adequately control the ailment, or possibly avoid it, when it is diagnosed in its early stages.

What is Diabetes?

Diabetes mellitus is a disease which affects the metabolic functions of the body. The carbohydrate intake of the body fails to "burn" properly and an excess of glucose accumulates in the bloodstream. This condition is known as hyperglycemia. The excess glucose is drained away in the urine and this condition is known as glycosuria.

Carbohydrates are the starch and sugar foods on which the body depends for its main source of energy. Foods are used immediately to supply heat and energy or they may be stored in the body for future use. In normal functioning the body makes use of these carbohydrates, but in diabetes this is not the case. The inability of the body to ulitize certain foods causes the excess glucose to accumulate in the blood and the kidneys to work overtime to excrete the sugar by way of the urine. In this light, diabetes may be considered more a condition than a disease, since it is not something one "catches."

Discovery of Insulin

A scientist named Paul Langerhans discovered a cluster of cells in the pancreas which were unlike the other tissues of the organ. Although this section of the pancreas bears his name, the islets of Langerhans, the significance of these cells was not known for some time after the discovery. It is the pancreas which secretes the necessary elements for utilization of the carbohydrates in the body. In 1921, F. G. Banting, a Canadian doctor, and C. H. Best, a graduate medical student, discovered insulin. It is this hormone, produced in the islets of Langerhans, that makes it possible for the body to convert the starches and sugars into the heat and energy it needs. Inadequate or faulty conversion of these substances can result in an imbalance between the food that is eaten and the metabolic needs of the body. The diabetic has the foods present but cannot use them. Since the body must have energy to live it turns on itself, developing poisons in the system that give rise to coma and eventually death. Untreated with insulin, or one of the newer oral drugs, diabetes is fatal.

Symptoms

Since the kidneys are working overtime to remove the excess sugar from the blood of the diabetic, he is likely to urinate frequently. This constant fluid loss from the body causes excessive thirst. It is likely that he will also be weak, listless, and hungry. The food he eats is not properly assimilated by the body; hence the diabetic may begin to lose weight no matter how much food he consumes. Other symptoms related to the imbalance in his system may be changes in vision, slow healing process, itching, pain in the fingers and toes, and/or drowsiness.

In less severe cases, only a few of these symptoms may occur. In fact, the diabetic is usually overweight for a time before a noticeable weight loss begins. In many cases, diabetes is discovered before any of these symptoms appear if the person undergoes a regular medical checkup.

Education

Special schools are not required for the diabetic child, but patient and understanding teachers are definitely an asset. The nature of diabetes in childhood may require mid-morning snacks to prevent insulin reactions. The erratic spilling of sugar into the urine may necessitate frequent trips from the classroom. Such manifestations may prove painfully embarrassing to the already sensitive child and cause humiliation before a class. An understanding teacher can handle such situations with a minimum of embarrassment to the child.

As the diabetic child progresses to the upper grades, this symptom-sensitivity lessens and the problem becomes more one of scheduling. Physical education classes must be arranged so that they will not place excessive strain on his insulinogenic functions. Teachers are often poorly informed or shamefully ignorant of the symptoms and control of diabetes and its accompanying problems. Although some teachers make an effort to learn about the needs of their diabetic students, it is frequently beneficial to have a doctor's statement of the child's specific medical needs and his ability to participate in sports or other forms of exercise.

The greatest problem for the teacher of an insulin-dependent diabetic is recognizing and counteracting insulin reaction. A teacher can provide additional support to the child's normal group adjustment by being aware, informed, and prepared for emergencies.

TUBERCULOSIS

Tuberculosis is one of the oldest diseases known to man. Evidence of tuberculosis has been found in Egyptian mummies dating as far back as 1000 B.C. The "white plague" has killed millions of humans within recorded history. Wars, famines, and pestilences have not equalled its terrible toll of dead and sick. For centuries it has been one of the world's biggest killers.

Today medical science has the means to eradicate this dreadful disease. It can be eliminated as a major public health problem in the United States through the application of modern-day techniques. It is recognized that this multifaceted program will take many years and will have to have intermediate goals along the way.

In the United States there are an estimated 25,000,000 people who have been infected by tubercle bacilli. While they are not sick, they have living TB germs in their bodies and may develop the active disease. Over a million and a half of these have actually been ill with the disease. An estimated two million will develop it in their lifetime unless it is prevented. Today approximately 250,000 Americans have active tuberculosis; another 550,000 have the disease in an inactive form and should be under medical supervision. In 1969, for example, there were 4,729 known cases of tuberculosis in the small state of Arkansas, 563 of which were newly reported cases.

Tuberculosis is more prevalent in urban slums because it spreads easily in a crowded, poorly ventilated environment. The infection rate for school entrants runs as high as 3 percent in some slum areas, whereas the national average is 0.3 percent (Tuberculosis in the U.S., 1969). But the well-housed, well-fed get TB, too. So do suburbanites and country folk. People of any age are susceptible.

Unlike other infectious and communicable disease, tuberculosis infection is not an active sickness, but it can become so. A person may be infected as long as forty or more years before the disease becomes active. More new cases in the next few years will be people who are now infected. Also, immunity is not acquired by having tuberculosis. Even though recovered, the tuberculosis victim may have a relapse.

Tuberculosis is primarily an airborne infectious disease caused by the tubercle bacillus (*Mycobacterium tuberculosis*). Persons become infected by breathing germs from an infectious patient. TB germs get into the air in contaminated droplets which are coughed, sneezed, talked, or laughed by a person with active tuberculosis. One cough may broadcast thousands of germs. They can be spread by contaminated articles, too. The natural defenses of the upper respiratory tract will filter out many of these germs, but some will get by and into the lungs. However, it usually takes prolonged exposure to an active case to become infected.

The lungs are a favorite spot of attack by TB germs, but they may strike any part of the body. The body counters with white cells which attempt to surround and destroy the germs. While the white cells are killing some germs, the body tries to enclose the invaders with a wall of cells and fibers. This reaction of the body creates a tiny lump called a tubercle that gives the disease its name. These form six to eight weeks after the initial entry and slow down the bacilli. At first the tubercle is soft and looks fuzzy, but it gradually hardens into a scar. Millions of people go through life with tubercles containing live germs in their lungs without ever getting sick.

Children with tuberculosis of the bones or joints will require a program consisting of relative physical inactivity for a long period of time. The number of children so afflicted has been reduced because of new drugs and surgical procedures. Children having tuberculosis will have the need to attend hospital schools and will later need home instruction. After the condition has been arrested the child will return to the regular classroom.

ALLERGIES

Eyes watery? Feel a sneeze coming on? Hand itching? If so, then you may be allergic to the paper you are holding. People are allergic to paper, the dust that may have accumulated on the edges of a book, or anything under the sun—including the sun itself.

If one can be allergic to anything, then just what is an allergy? Allergy is an acquired, specific, altered capability to react, based on an antigen-antibody reaction (Harris and Shure, 1969). Most of us can eat bananas, strawberries, or other foods without any worry. Most of us can breathe house dust without problems, but those who do have these problems are showing an "altered" or unusual reaction.

An antigen is a substance which enters the body and triggers the allergic reaction and allergic symptoms. Allergen is often used as a synonym for antigen. Some common antigens are house dust, pollen, feathers, and mold, but as was previously stated, they may be anything from the living room carpet to the kitchen sink cleanser. Antigens may enter the body through touch, inhalation, or ingestion. Antigens are either complete or incomplete. A complete antigen is able to produce antibodies and to unite with them to cause the allergic reaction. Incomplete antigens cannot perform both functions.

Do you know the most common allergy problems? If hay fever came quickly to mind, then you are correct; some other common allergies are bronchial asthma, eczema, urticaria or hives, insect, and drug allergies. Let's take a closer look at these common allergies—their causes and treament.

Hay Fever

During the seventeenth century doctors thought the symptoms of sneezing, runny nose, and watery eyes were brought on by an emotional upset. For a long time afterward the same symptoms occurring during rose-blooming time were called "rose fever." Even later these same symptoms occurring during the haying season in England came to be called "hay fever." Although it is scientifically incorrect, the name has persisted. The correct name is allergic rhinitis.

Bronchial Asthma

Bottomley (1968) characterizes bronchial asthma as a clinically recognizable type of wheezing and difficulty in breathing which is caused by narrowing of the smallest branches of the bronchial tubes throughout both lungs, and by the presence of tenacious mucus in these smallest branches. Often in its early stages it occurs as isolated attacks which are relieved by adrenalin or related drugs and are reversible. Asthma attacks brought on by factors outside the body are said to have extrinsic causes. Intrinsic causes are those which stem from inside the body. Extrinsic causes include medicines, food, or pollen, while intrinsic causes might be infections or a highly disturbed emotional state.

Skin Allergies

The skin is one of the largest and most important organs of the body. It is also one the most sensitive organs and is vulnerable to allergic reactions through touch or through the bloodstream. The most common skin allergies are hives (urticaria) and eczema (atopic dermatitis).

Hives consist of white or reddish wheals and welts which itch, sting, and prick. Hives may attack a specific area of the body or spread over all areas. The trunk, buttocks, and chest are the parts of the body most frequently affected. Sometimes hives are combined with other diseases such as eczema. Causes of hives include bacteria from infections in any part of the body, foods, drugs, inhalants in any season, time, or place, contactants of any sort, and the elements of heat, wind, light, or cold.

Reactions to Biting and Stinging Insects

It is normal to experience localized swelling, redness, and itching following the bite or sting of an insect. It is abnormal to experience flushing and swelling of the face and neck, fits of sneezing, watering of the eyes, coughing, and difficulty in breathing. These symptoms constitute an altered or allergic reaction to insect stings and bites.

Drug Allergies

Although it is expected that drugs will cause a reaction in the body of the user, an unusual and unexpected reaction to a particular drug is an allergic reaction. Drugs are powerful foreign substances to which the body is not accustomed and should naturally be used with extreme care. The United States Food and Drug Administration has strict labeling laws regarding possible adverse reactions to nonprescription medications. Doctors and pharmacists are well-informed about prescription drugs.

Most children suffering from allergies will not need special educational planning unless they are hospitalized or home-bound. The regular classroom teacher must be constantly alerted to the fact that if a child has an allergic attack the home should be notified immediately. If the child does not have other disabilities which hinder educational achievement, he will be able to participate like normal children.

RHEUMATIC FEVER

Rheumatic fever ranks as one of the major infectious diseases of childhood and early adolescence. Though it is not the dreaded disease that it has been in the past, it still creates many serious health problems. The associated problems of a rheumatic heart account for about fifty thousand deaths per year in the United States. Its prevention and treatment continue to present a challenge to the medical profession.

Definition and Etiology

Rheumatic fever is a chronic inflammatory disease which is characterized by fever and swelling of the joints. The exact pathogenesis of the disease is not known, but it has been observed that it follows infection with group A beta-hemolytic streptococcus. Studies on selected populations have shown that 3 percent of individuals with untreated group A streptococcal infection will develop rheumatic fever (Hughes, 1967).

Many mild cases of rheumatic fever occur and are unrecognized. This mild condition in children is often called growing pains. However, the pains of these two conditions can be distinguished by noting that generally growing pains are in the muscles and occur at night. The pain of rheumatic fever is in the joints. The name "rheumatic fever" emphasizes the inflamed condition of the joints. This, however, is of secondary importance. The most serious implication of rheumatic fever is involvement of the heart. This condition could lead to permanent disability or death.

The original infection of group A streptococcus is usually mild and the resulting rheumatic fever may not cause heart damage. However, reinfection is common and often more severe. The frequent result of reinfection is damage to the heart.

The sequence in rheumatic fever ordinarily follows a pattern of three steps. There is an initial infection with group A beta-hemolytic streptococcus such as is present in scarlet fever, respiratory tract infections, and sore throat. This is followed by a latent period of one to three weeks. The third step is the onset of rheumatic fever.

Incidence

Rheumatic fever is primarily a disease of childhood which occurs chiefly between the ages of five and fifteen. The disease is rare in the first four years of life and becomes rare again during the adult years. The high incidence of streptococcal infection during childhood and early adolescence would seem directly related. When there is a high incidence of streptococcal infection in the adult population, an outbreak of rheumatic fever is a common result.

There are no reliable figures which give the incidence of rheumatic fever in the general population. The disease is not always recognized and reported to a physician. Commonly used as a reasonable index is the incidence of 3 percent of the untreated streptococcal cases. This has been decreasing for several years as has the incidence of streptococcal infection. The associated problems of rheumatic heart disease present the more serious problems.

As implied previously, all children who have rheumatic fever do not have rheumatic heart disease, and all children who have had heart murmurs are not necessarily ill. Rheumatic fever is serious because it generally requires long periods of convalescence and is responsible for approximately 90 percent of the defective hearts in children. All teachers should be alerted to the symptoms of rheumatic fever.

After an attack, the period of treatment during convalescence may be long. During this time the child will need a great deal of parental support and also home instruction from an itinerant teacher.

When the child returns to the regular classroom, there will be a few adjustments in curriculum and various types of activities permitted. However, the teacher's greatest responsibility is the prevention of reinfection and not a limitation of physical activity. The American Heart Association (1963) lists the following classifications which most physicians will refer to the school:

FUNCTIONAL CAPACITY

Class I. Patients with cardiac disease, but without resulting limitation of physical activity. Ordinary physical activity does not cause undue fatigue, palpitation, dyspnea or anginal pain.

Class II. Patients with cardiac disease resulting in slight limitation of physical activity. They are comfortable at rest. Ordinary physical activity results in fatigue, palpitation, dyspnea or anginal pain.

Class III. Patients with cardiac disease resulting in marked limitation of physical activity. They are comfortable at rest. Less than ordinary activity causes fatigue, palpitation, dyspnea or anginal pain.

Class IV. Patients with cardiac disease resulting in inability to carry on any physical activity without discomfort. Symptoms of cardiac insufficiency or of the anginal syndrome may be present even at rest. If any physical activity is undertaken discomfort is increased.

THERAPEUTIC CLASSIFICATION

Class A. Patients with cardiac disease whose physical activity need not be restricted.

Class B. Patients with cardiac disease whose ordinary physical activity need not be restricted, but who should be advised against severe or competitive physical efforts.

Class C. Patients with cardiac disease whose ordinary physical activity should be moderately restricted, and whose more strenuous efforts should be discontinued.

Class D. Patients with cardiac disease whose ordinary physical activity should be markedly restricted.

Class E. Patients with cardiac disease who should be at complete rest, confined to bed or chair.

EPILEPSY

Epileptic children are discussed in this chapter since this condition is a cerebral dysfunction. This is a condition which requires medication and management rather than physical habilitation.

Epilepsy is a frightening condition because of the nature of the seizures. The best-known seizure is the grand mal type, the convulsion in which the individual falls and becomes unconscious. In petit mal the individual loses consciousness only momentarily. There is no convulsion of the body but the eyes stare and the eyelids twitch. In psychomotor epilepsy one usually has short periods of amnesia. One stares, drops things, mumbles, and does not remember his actions. Jacksonian epilepsy begins with a convulsion of one side of the body, usually starting at the foot and working up to the arm.

The advance of medicine has made it possible for most epileptic children to remain in the regular classroom. The convulsions can be controlled by medication in 80 percent of the cases of epilepsy.

Epilepsy, like other defects and diseases, exists in varying degrees. One individual may be affected only mildly with a great time-lapse between seizures while another one may have very frequent, violent attacks; and then there are others who will range between these extremes. This may be the only problem of the individual or may be one of many. Most attacks can be controlled by medication and the individual affected is more normal than not.

Causes, Age at Onset, Predisposing Factors

It seems that no one is sure as to the exact cause of epilepsy, but there does seem to be general agreement that the seizures are caused by some chemical reaction within the brain that affects the nerves and muscles. A great deal of study has been done as to why some people are susceptible. Most authorities think that there has been an injury to some part of the brain that could have happened during the prenatal, paranatal, or postnatal periods.

Prenatal causes could be hereditary, parental infections, anoxia, injury to the brain, diabetes, and excessive x-ray. Paranatal factors could be anoxia, injury by forceps, prolonged labor, Rh factor, and prematurity. Postnatal causes could arise from anoxia, trauma, infections, tumors, and injuries caused by accidents.

With some epileptics there seem to be precipitating factors that cause seizures. Some of these factors are emotional shock, childhood fears, parental and peer rejection, and severe frustrations.

If the child's seizures are controlled, and he is not multiply handicapped, then he can function adequately in the regular classroom. Even if the child should have a seizure, the regular class teacher should know what to do in an emergency. First of all, the teacher should remain calm and not frighten the children. Next, she should turn the child's head to the side so that he will not choke on saliva, and she should make such that the child does not swallow his tongue. Again, it should be pointed out that if the child's intelligence is not severely impaired, he should have no problem functioning in the regular classroom.

CYSTIC FIBROSIS

Cystic fibrosis is a congenital, inherited disease affecting the pancreas, respiratory system, and sweat glands. It usually begins in infancy, and is typified by chronic respiratory infection, pancreatic insufficiency, and susceptibility to heat prostration. This condition is the leading cause of chronic lung disease in American babies and affects about one out of every eight hundred. Caucasians are the primary race to suffer from cystic fibrosis and a few American Negroes suffer from the disease. However, it is a very rare occurrence in Orientals.

More and more people are becoming aware of this disease through the National Cystic Fibrosis Foundation in New York. This organization publishes many leaflets and booklets each year concerning this disease.

Cystic fibrosis may occur in either sex, and it is inherited from both sides of the family. If only one parent carries the gene for cystic fibrosis, that parent will have no symptoms. If he has children, there will be a fifty-fifty chance that these children will be carriers of the recessive gene but none will have the disease or any of the symptoms. However, if both parents carry the gene, each child will have a one-in-four chance of having cystic fibrosis. Not many years ago, cystic fibrosis was confined to infancy and early childhood because the disease resulted in early death. Now these individuals often live to thirty-five or forty years of age and even older. They often function as normal human beings and have children who do not have the disease.

It is believed that in the United States, there are over ten million people who carry the recessive gene for cystic fibrosis. The odds are twenty to one that any one person is a carrier of the gene. People can have tests made to detect if they are carriers.

It was not many years ago that cystic fibrosis was considered a rare but fatal disease. Now it is recognized as a very common disease and it is known that patients can lead a rewarding life if the condition is discovered early.

Almost all of the exocrine glands of an individual with

cystic fibrosis are affected to some degree of severity. In all cases the sweat of the diseased person has a high level of salt. Because of this high salt content, large amounts of salt are lost from the body.

The main sources of complications are the mucous glands. These secrete abnormally thick, gluey mucus. In a normal adult, the mucus is thin and slippery, and it helps keep air passages clear by carrying off dust particles and germs. In a person suffering from cystic fibrosis the air passages become clogged because of the thick mucus. It is possible that his digestion, lungs, and liver may also be affected.

Education

The child with cystic fibrosis will be under the care of a physician. The teacher must be aware that the child does not have a communicable disease, also that his energy level is not as high as that of the other children and therefore he will fatigue easier than the other children. Knowing these things, the teacher in the regular classroom can help the child to carry on a fairly normal existence. The teacher will also need to work very closely with the child's parents to know of any changes in the child's condition and also to help the parents teach the child at home during convalescence.

Because of the tremendous scientific strides that have been made concerning the control of cystic fibrosis, most children having this disease can be educated in the regular classroom, assuming they do not have other handicapping conditions. These children will miss school more than the average and possible a home-bound teacher will be consulted periodically.

One big problem that the teacher will face will be the peer disapproval of the child with cystic fibrosis. The teacher must ever strive to insure that the other children do not think that the apparent respiratory ailment is communicable.

REFERENCES

Bottomley, H. W.: *Allergy: Its Treatment and Care.* New York, Funk & Wagnalls, 1968.

Harris, M. C., and Shure, N.: *All About Allergy.* Englewood Cliffs, N. J., Prentice-Hall, 1969.

Hughes, J. G.: *Synopsis of Pediatrics*, 2nd ed. St. Louis, C. V. Mosby, 1967.

New York Heart Association: *Nomenclature and Criteria for Diagnosis of Disease of the Heart and Blood Vessels*, 5th ed. New York, The New York Heart Association, 1963.

Chapter 11

CLASSROOM ECOLOGY

SPECIAL CLASSES

IT IS ONLY natural that efforts to treat divergent educational needs led to the compartmentalization of segments of the school population. Thus the recognition that certain children were unable to compete in regular classroom situations prompted the creation of special education classes. These classes, for the most part, were for children who were referred to as mentally retarded, emotionally disturbed, or suffering from various other handicapping conditions. These classes served as springboards for the creation of other programs for specific groups of children— "gifted," "average," "below average," and for "children from disadvantaged backgrounds." The variety of abilities and interests in classroom situations suggested that greater instructional efficiency would result if children were grouped according to ability. Such grouping was viewed as a means of restricting the range of talents with which a teacher must deal, of enabling teachers to base standards on anticipated performance levels, and of placing students with special learning problems in classrooms managed by teachers with specialized training.

At first glance, it seems plausible that special classes should be established and special programs created. However, it is time that other approaches be considered. Special classes and special programs are justified on the basis that, without them, children are unable for various reasons to compete with other children. The question which needs to be asked is, "Compete

---

Note—The idea for this chapter is taken from *Early Childhood Education* by Harold D. Love and William H. Osborne (Springfield, Thomas, 1971). Parts of this chapter are taken from *Early Childhood Education* with the permission of authors and publisher.

on what basis?" If competition is based on ability to meet unitary standards in classrooms, it is suggested that it is infinitely more appropriate to alter classroom standards than to create special programs for children to whom the standards do not apply. The author suggests that since we now accept the fact that there exists a diversity of needs, attitudes, and interests in our society, we should focus our efforts to permit these diversities to exist in regular classroom environments .

The attempts to restrict regular classrooms to children who can compete with respect to single standards deny the multifarious standards of the community. Education should spend less time creating "special programs" for "special students" and devote its energies and resources toward the creation of classroom environments which allow for the broad range of learning, behavioral needs, and interests of students. This would emphasize that all children have as much value in the classroom as they do in society at large.

Homogeneous Grouping

Homogeneous grouping recognizes the process of progressive achievement decrement—the process wherein students who are behind when they enter the first grade tend to be further behind at the end of the second, still further behind at the end of the third, and ultimately so far behind that withdrawal from school is often the only alternative. Usually grouping is based on some assessment of achievement level, and those who "test out" at equivalent levels are placed in the same group.

Certain conclusions are then drawn concerning each group. The lower group, for example, is usually assumed to be behind. This poses a problem because the teacher is likely to develop the expectancy that the "behind group" is likely to remain so. This raises the paradox wherein children are placed in a group in order for them to correct "deficiencies," but the nature of selection and the concomitant teacher attitude may reduce the chance the group will overcome these deficiencies. It is therefore possible that the grouping process will contribute to the very problem it is designed to solve.

The idea that students can be grouped into homogeneous units is more of a myth than a reality. It is a myth because grouping techniques merely control certain variables, and the effectiveness of this control is open to question. Grouping based on achievement-test results postulates the accuracy of the tests, assumes that background experiences are constant, and that questions mean the same thing to all persons who are writing the examination. Since these assumptions may not be valid, it follows that decisions based on them may be invalid.

Even if it is possible to control the variables which determine group assignment, the group is still not homogeneous with respect to factors which underlie achievement—interests, motivation, parental attitudes, peer acceptance, social class status, and a variety of other factors too numerous to mention.

The point is that we assume groups to be homogeneous because of performance levels on some criterion (perhaps even criteria), but that in reality the group is heterogeneous. Educational programs based on the assumption of homogeneity of a group can therefore be challenged rather seriously as to appropriateness to the needs of individual children.

It appears that homogeneous grouping was a response to a need, but that it was an inaccurate response and more viable alternatives are mandated. Unfortunately, however, it appears that efforts to categorize students are on the increase. From a historical perspective, we have tended to identify groups and develop crash programs to solve the problems we thought existed. Thus we discovered "juvenile delinquents" and set up programs for them, "emotionally disturbed" and set up programs for them, "mentally retarded" and set up programs for them, "gifted" and set up "enrichment" programs for them. Now we have programs for "disadvantaged children." It is as if we discovered all at once that there were poor people and that something needed doing.

Target schools were identified, special teacher training programs were instituted, and the effort to correct educational deficiencies was launched. The effort accepted the validity of the main thrust of educational programs—preparation for college admission—and programs for the disadvantaged were slanted toward remedial or compensatory efforts so these students could, along with all others, be ready for college admission.

The author argues that programs should not be designed, for example, to provide remedial or compensatory assistance to disadvantaged students so they can overcome certain academic deficiencies or meet the standards or requirements of the educational system, but rather that all programs should be based on the need to assist all students to come to better grips with real life situations. Such programs should attempt to assist children to learn and develop skills so they can enrich their lives, rather than attempt to lull children into a pattern wherein they can conform to some single classroom standard.

More specifically, it is believed that the current practice—to dichotomize school populations into disadvantaged and nondisadvantaged groups and treat them accordingly—poses more problems than solutions.

Implications

The practice of placing students in special classes and homogeneous groupings has the following implications:

1. The practice implies that the groups are uniform or homogeneous—that is, by the mere fact that children meet certain economic criteria, they possess similar learning and behavioral needs. Moreover, programs for children from economically deprived backgrounds seem to reflect an attitude that failure is the manifest destiny of these children. Further, it appears an attitude prevails to the effect that, after failure occurs, then, and apparently only then, the school can do something about it—through remedial or compensatory programs.

2. The practice suggests that little or no interaction should transpire between the two groups. This is especially interesting if such claims as, "Disadvantaged children have limited communication skills, are present-oriented, respond only to sounds of authority," and a host of other factors are true. It is also interesting because these factors seem to suggest that interaction among groups will be of significant value.

3. The practice assumes that academically oriented educational programs for nondisadvantaged children are appropriate.

This is said because the main thrust of remedial and compensatory programs for the disadvantaged is to assist them in coping with academically oriented programs. Thus we know the typical school program produces failure (parenthetically, we do not really know if it produces success), and we react by treating its failures—not the process which produced these failures—unlike most other treatment programs, which seek to discover and correct causes rather than treat symptoms.

4. The practice assumes programs for nondisadvantaged children are adequately financed. We draw this conclusion from the comparison of federal expenditures for educational programs for the disadvantaged with expenditures for activities related to the total educational process (library, educational media, teacher salaries, equipment, and so forth).

5. Since the practice concentrates on failures (i.e. "waste products"), the element of accountability is removed from the educational system. As long as education is not compelled to examine why failures exist, or as long as it is permitted to shift blame to children for its limitations, then for that long can the system avoid looking into itself to discover why children drop out, lose interest, cease being creative, and turn to other means, such as drugs, in order to be "turned on." It is true that educators, particularly administrators, must report to school boards and to various elements of the community. In the process, however, they overlook accountability for treating students with dignity and respect, for providing programs so that even the "weakest" have a vital part to play, and for providing growth-fostering environments.

Higher education is also in line for the charge that it operates in a splendid absence of accountability. Prospective teachers are taught by instructors who have long forgotten what classrooms (both local schools and their own) are all about. Admission to the "professional" aspect of teacher preparatory programs is centered on how well the student has responded to the system and, in the process, disregards how well the system has responded to the student.

When one considers the rigidity of education departments toward change, it is of little wonder that local schools are also rigid. When one considers how little time is spent in permitting prospective teachers to deal with children in real situations, it becomes understandable that the educational system feels itself competent to tell a six-year-old child he is a failure, immature, a slow learner, and a host of other things.

These five points lead to the contention that education should not categorize students on the facility of these students to compete with the educational program as it currently operates.

Alternatively, it is maintained that classrooms and schools are microcosms of society, and that the divergency and differences which exist in society have correlates in classroom and school environments. Consequently the educational system should ensure that classroom activities are germane to a variety of interests, learning, and behavioral needs. Further, differences among students in classrooms are not only to be tolerated but in fact encouraged. In addition, it is claimed that children differ at various grade levels, and that performance at subsequent grade levels is contingent, in large part, on exposure and experiences at preceding grade levels.

One can almost draw the inference that educators assume, because of the unbelievable progress made in science and math, that they know best what a child should learn, when he should learn it, and how he should go about learning it. Further, it appears that educators operate on the premise that not only do they know these things, but they are the only ones who do. This position ignores the significance of learning which occurred before the child entered school, the intensity of his motivation to learn, and the frequency with which children, as they progress through the educational system, lose their desire to learn.

The school is concerned about developing communication skills, and it does this by insisting that children be quiet and not talk to one another.

The school attempts to develop social skills, and it does this by preventing social interaction—except at periodic intervals.

The school is interested in fostering a desire in children to learn, and it does this through drill and other repetitive techniques which can easily discourage motivation.

The school is designed to assist the student to become an

individual in his own right, and it does this by forcing him to adhere to a group standard.

The school hopes to "produce" warm and humanistic children, and it does this by sometimes subjecting children who are warm, honest, and humanistic to treatment by cool and impersonal teachers.

The school is designed to assist children to understand the unique value of themselves and other children, and it does this by offering programs which exclude systemically a number of students.

The school is to provide a growth-nurturing environment which permits the child to learn from experiences, and it does this by insisting that "right," and only "right," answers be given.

Teacher training programs mention the importance of parental attitudes on children's behavior, and they emphasize this importance by failing to include any exposure to parents in the teacher training curricula.

Emphasis is placed on the teacher as a warm and understanding human being, and this emphasis is met in teacher preparatory programs by more and more insistence on subject-matter mastery, and less and less attention to interpersonal relationship skills.

Educational psychology courses emphasize the uniqueness of individuals, and this uniqueness is expressed in other courses by emphasis on tricks of the trade which prevent children from deviating from the norm.

These criticisms are made even though there is an awareness that alternatives must be suggested. The author is not presumptuous enough to believe that people who are critical of education practices can recast the educational structure. It is hoped, however, that we can interest other people in the effort because a ground swell of public opinion is needed. After all, it took a long time and a lot of people to get us to our present state.

Ecological Significance

"Classroom ecology" is a phrase which is being used more and more frequently. Its implications can be of particular benefit to educational programs, provided the significance of the phrase is fully understood.

Ecology implies that systems of life are influenced and modified by other systems of life (i.e. life does not exist in isolated compartments, and alterations in one life form produce changes in other forms). One can see in nature the interdependence of life systems on one another and the impact on all other systems as the result of interferences with one system. For example, in certain areas, there has been a rapid increase in the number of rabbits because of programs which led to the destruction of natural enemies of rabbits. This increase had effects on other systems which influenced still other systems.

Classroom ecology reflects an awareness that a variety of life systems also exist within classroom situations and implies that treatment of one system at the expense of others can produce classroom imbalances analogous to those produced in nature. Conversely, it implies that a classroom environment which provides favorable treatment for all life systems therein will produce positive results greater than would be obtained if the same treatments were applied separately to individual groups. Expressed in more concrete terms, for example, the enrichment of educational opportunities for both gifted and nongifted children in a classroom will produce greater benefits to both groups than separate enrichment would offer.

Nature suggests that without the smallest life forms eventually the largest forms would perish, and that without the largest forms the smallest forms would also perish. We are becoming more aware of this phenomenon in nature and are responding by increased emphasis on conservation, control of pollution, and so on.

Since we are experiencing the impact, we realize that social imbalances have been created—for example, the fear which developed shortly after Sputnik was launched that we were producing too few scientists and mathematicians. We were less concerned about the need for political and social scientists. The result is that the shift from a technological to a political and social crisis finds us with a shortage of competent persons in social and political science. Thus we are not prepared to deal with problems we now face. The question is, however, will our response to the current crisis be such that we will overlook or deemphasize programs which train persons to treat other crises which undoubtedly will arise?

The apparent need for more engineers, mathematicians, and other scientific personnel contributed to the demand for more guidance and universities. This contributed to the situation wherein more students sought admission to institutions of higher education and fewer elected to pursue programs of study necessary to gain technological competence. It appeared the only way to earn a ticket to the "good life" was through a college degree.

School populations were divided into two groups, those who would attend college and those who would not. Even though the latter group was larger in number, the bulk of educational dollars was expended to support programs for the former. This and other factors contributed to the present circumstances where there is a shortage of skilled labor, a surplus of persons who are without skills (potentially, there may be a time when there is a surplus of persons with academic training), and we appear to be approaching the time when it will be almost cheaper to purchase a new appliance than it is to have it repaired.

Certain other decisions have been made with respect to educational needs of selected groups. For example, available vocational subjects appear to be reserved for "slow learners" and the like, and, intentionally or accidentally, are scheduled at times which conflict with academic courses. Pursuit of academic training thereby prevents a number of students from learning to use tools or master other basic vocational skills. At the same time, vocational courses seem to be held in low regard and are viewed as the domain of those who could not do anything else. The low priority given to vocational subjects in schools usually means that, in periods of financial crisis, these subjects are the last to be developed and the first to be eliminated. As a consequence students who, for a variety of reasons, do not elect to pursue further academic training find there is nothing in school programs relevant to their needs or appropriate to their present circumstances. These students withdraw from school and seek employment in unskilled or semiskilled occupations. Subsequent efforts to train them to enter skilled occupations are extremely expensive, and at this time the efficiency of vocational training programs to meet job demands is questionable.

We have learned that the negative impact of environmental alterations can be reduced, provided the environment is permitted (in many cases, "treated") to approximate its original integrity. For example, pollution of streams, rivers, and lakes can be reduced, the use of various pesticides eliminated, game perserves established, new reefs created in oceans, and a variety of other conservation programs instituted.

Similar measures can be adopted for educational programs. That is, we can attempt to correct social environmental problems. If the poverty cycle is perpetrated because persons within the cycle have not been provided the skills, techniques, or hope they need if they are to escape, it seems reasonable for us to develop procedures whereby these needs are provided for. We have, in fact, attempted to do this through the "war on poverty." (When this war is evaluated, we will probably find it to be the first war the United States has ever lost.)

Compensatory programs have been attempted, evaluated, and regarded as successful or unsuccessful—depending on the point of view of those who do the evaluation, and those who read the reports. Still, there seems to be an uneasy consensus among people that compensatory programs are not producing the results which are expected. Many reasons—"differences in intelligence levels among races," "compensatory programs are basically racist," "inadequate financial support"—have been advanced in order to explain the shortcomings of compensatory programs. Our concern is that most criticism overlooks the rationale, the structure, and the content of compensatory programs. It is almost as if the compensatory programs are felt to be appropriate, and that therefore the cause of failure must reside elsewhere.

It is evident, then, that when we attempt to explain shortcomings in compensatory programs, we use the same reasons we use when explaining the shortcomings in regular programs. This poses some interesting quesetions. Since, for the most part, students in compensatory programs are "homogeneous" with respect to economic backgrounds, it is possible that separation of "disadvantaged" children from "nondisadvantaged" children is an ineffective strategy? Or is it possible that we are so locked into an academic orientation that we do not know how to evaluate programs? The answer to both of these must be "no." Otherwise, (1) we would not continue to pour money into programs specifically for disadvantaged children, and (2) "evaluation" would not be the "hottest buzz-word going."

We believe compensatory educational programs can serve to stimulate learning and meet behavioral needs if certain conditions are met:

1. The word "compensatory" should be dropped. This is essential in order to eliminate feelings that only children who are failing are assigned to these programs.

2. Teachers, administrators, and the community must analyze their own feelings in the matter. Regardless of name changes and such, behavioral objectives—explicit and implicit, must be reviewed and expectancies—explicit and implicit, must be known. Without these analyses, program managers are apt to continue to maintain the position that, in the last analysis, the program is for persons who do not measure up.

3. The attitude that assignment to these programs must be reserved for a select group must be changed.

4. Curricula should be based on learning and behavioral needs of all students.

5. Divergencies in background experiences and needs must be accepted.

6. The present emphasis on procedures and strategies, rather than students, should be shifted back to students; and any blame for failure should be shifted from children to program.

Our position in stating the above is to insist that compensatory educational programs have not produced the results which were hoped for because certain conclusions were drawn with respect to the impact of environmental circumstances of children. It was implied that the only way to "improve their life styles" was through the rejection of "bad" environments. The problem with this is that a child's environment is real, whereas the reality of classroom programs is open to question.

We suggest the alternative is to eliminate judgments based

on environmental circumstances, utilize real things students encounter in their lives as instructional devices, and grant students the right to make decisions concerning what they feel is appropriate and inappropriate to their personal lives.

The reader may question, then, the difference between compensatory education, as we discuss it, and the rest of the educational system. Our response is that there is no difference, and that the addition of "compensatory" education programs as separate and distinct units from "regular" educational programs indicates shortcomings in the total educational system which must be corrected. In our haste and intention to produce "well-educated people," we have ruled out a number of children. We must now institute steps to bring them back in, or else face the reality that whatever balance does exist in classrooms is in danger of being lost. By ignoring the individuality of children, and by subjecting them to the same set of standards, expectancies, and judgments, and then evaluating them, we have, in education, minimized certain environments. At the same time, we do not provide inhabitants of these environments with the skills they need to cope with other environments.

If we are concerned with classroom ecology, as well we should be, we must adopt an educational position which is founded on an honest desire to utilize multiple teaching strategies appropriate to multiple standards. In such classrooms, all children—advantaged and disadvantaged, gifted and retarded, healthy and crippled—are inseparable parts of a whole. Thus each child assumes an important role in the class because he conforms to some classification system and not because he comes from a certain background.

In nature, there is an interaction among the different forms of animal and plant life. There is also interaction among children in schools and classrooms. Both interactions are modifiable as the result of environmental influences. The diversity of systems in nature leads to a common goal, namely, an improved opportunity for learning and behavioral needs to be met.

We are certain every teacher and every administrator has heard at least once in his professional career that each child is a unique being. We expect that most teachers discover classrooms are composed of individual children presenting individual differences. It is a pity we ignore what we see.

Instead of basing instructional patterns and strategies on what we know to be correct, we base them on the assumption that the class is a unit. Also, we assume children in the unit have as little interest in learning as we do. We fail to remember that at some point in the past we, too, were intensely interested in learning, but somewhere along the way we lost the urge; and we assist children to follow in our footsteps by treating them as we were treated.

Outside the school there is interaction among students, and they learn from it. They may, in fact, learn much more than they do in typical classrooms. It seems plausible, then, that we should not be reluctant to carry the playground into the schools. It may be noisy in schools if such interaction is permitted, but since when did silence become a virtue? After all, there is nothing more silent than the dead!

Since, regardless of efforts by adults to prevent it, children will relate to one another, it appears reasonable to include these relationships as integral parts of educational programs. If we accept this premise, we must also accept the corollary principle that the teacher's role must be changed in order to permit student participation in the entire spectrum of classroom activities —including planning.

Teacher preparatory programs must be changed if the full impact of the concept of classroom ecology is to be realized. This will be extremely difficult because, in the last analysis, teacher preparatory programs cut across the entire spectrum of academic offerings in a college or university. The quality of instruction has not been a significant issue in higher education, the relationship of general education courses to their avowed purposes (i.e. to produce well-educated people) is open to question, and there is a general reluctance in higher education to accept change. The burden of producing changes in teacher preparatory programs will thus fall on departments of education, and this certainly reduces the chances that any substantial changes will be made in the academic part of teacher preparatory programs. The possibility does exist, however, that education departments can implement programs which will enhance the ability of future teachers to relate to students.

Reasoning

We believe early experiences with children will enable us to develop alternative procedures for the following reasons:

1. We know a large number of freshmen students are forced, for various reasons, to leave college before they complete degree requirements. Given the opportunity, many of these students can assume important roles in schools, particularly if we change our point of view from individual classroom teachers to instructional teams. If freshman students work with children while under the supervision of teacher managers and college faculty members, they can become familiar with school and classroom management procedures as well as instructional principles. (In fact, the experiences students receive can be based on particular interests and learning needs they exhibit.) Therefore, students who withdraw from college prior to graduation will be qualified to enter various roles in schools. This differs from programs which are designed to train paraprofessionals in that the program makes "paraprofessional training" an integral part of the total teacher training process. More specifically, we feel paraprofessional training should constitute one "rung" of a "career ladder" training program. Making it a significant part of the teacher training process should result in an increase in the scope of activities these persons undertake. The fact that college students are being trained should permit the inclusion of more contact with children. This, in turn, should enable teachers to examine means whereby student interns can assume responsibility for various facets of the instructional process.

2. The involvement of student interns provides a joint opportunity for local schools and colleges to examine both teacher training procedures and concepts of the role of teachers in classroom management. We need clarification of what a teacher is supposed to do, when he should do it, and how it should be done, in light of the fact that our present procedures

are neither reducing class size nor enabling teachers to cope with the spectrum of learning and behavioral needs which exist in their classrooms. Hopefully, we will find it is possible to restructure the role of teachers, develop alternative educational strategies, and avoid the risk that the education system will price itself out of existence.

3. The variety of experiences or activities student interns are given can be ordered in such fashion that their involvement with children progresses as competence increases. Note the emphasis on competence rather than on time. We see no reason to base what student interns do on how they are classified in college (i.e. a student should engage in activities because he is ready, not because he is a freshman, sophomore, and so on).

4. Student interns will have the opportunity to be actively involved with children, and this involvement should be beneficial to both. Also, it enables college faculty members to include an assessment of the student intern's ability to relate to children when faculty reach the point where they must judge whether or not students should be permitted to continue in teacher preparatory programs. This is vastly different from the present situation where the principle determinant for recommendation for a certificate is the quality of performance in academic courses. This also provides prospective teachers with an opportunity to decide early in their college programs whether or not they want to enter the teaching profession. The number of persons who complete teacher training programs but who do not enter teaching, or who soon leave teaching, indicates the need for early decision making.

5. Students will have the opportunity to move in and out of the teacher training process. In this manner they can pursue interests they may have but which, under the present program, they must either ignore or delay.

6. College faculty members will have the opportunity to rediscover children and classrooms. This may be a traumatic experience for many, and this in itself indicates the need for experience.

There are many advantages to student involvement with

children. In the last analysis, though, we feel the most significant reason is that college students today really want to be involved. It will be a pity if we in education deny them this privilege.

Chapter 12

THE SPECIAL EDUCATION VIEWPOINT

IN A STATEMENT of policy concerning basic commitments to exceptional children by Reynolds, Willenberg, MacKinnon, and Voelker (1971) it was said that the right to an education for all is a democratic tradition which is reflected in our laws and educational practice, but that sometimes a commitment to this tradition in the case of children who have unique educational needs presents a real challenge to the schools of our country. Children who are exceptional are frequently unable to attain full education from the regular school system. There is no doubt that many children have needs such as very specialized diagnostic and instructional services, an opportunity to view themselves and others in a wholesome manner, and a need to experience community interaction with other people. This policy statement goes on to say that because of their exceptionality, many children need to begin their school experiences at an earlier age than most children in our society. Many individuals require services well into adulthood.

Reynolds *et al.* (1971) had this to say concerning the challenge that is reflected in the philosophy of education in America:

> There are at least five times as many school systems providing special educational services to exceptional children as there were a quarter of a century ago, although relatively few services exist for the intellectually gifted. In the regular education, there is a surge of interest in individualizing instruction which, hopefully, means more sensitivity to all children—and particularly to those with special needs. Despite these apparent gains, it has never been clearer that the schools are failing to understand and serve the individual needs of many children; less than half the children who need highly specialized services are receiving them.

There is no doubt that special education has grown rapidly.

There is still a need, however, to improve our educational services in many areas. We are now raising many fundamental questions concerning the roles of the schools and other educational agencies in educating exceptional children. We are asking about family rights with regard to the education of children. We are trying to determine if certain labels truly aid in perpetuating a disability. Many special educators think "yes" concerning the above-mentioned, and many special educators think "no" concerning this.

The Council for Exceptional Children has a policy statement (1971) which attempts to clarify a position for professional educators in the field of special education:

> Commitment to the principle of special education for all encompasses the responsibility to provide carefully individualized instruction to all children. This responsibility extends to children and youth wherever they may be, through all degrees and kinds of exceptionality, and to all individuals without regard to their potential ability to contribute to society.

This means that educational opportunities should not be denied to any child. Also, it means that the potentialities for a child making a contribution to society are not a requirement for him to enter school. Education is for all, and each individual should be provided the best education according to his capabilities, whether it be in a special classroom or the regular classroom. We should have a commitment in America to every child, which includes those with vision, speech, hearing, and learning problems; those from disadvantaged backgrounds; and those who are gifted. There is no doubt that providing education for these children requires a variety of specialized skills and services, and also that they are costly and often necessitate radical innovation. Very often we must get away from tradition to do what is best for these children. What is best for these children can be done in the regular clasroom but generally is not. This is why we now have and probably always will have special classes for exceptional children.

In the past any school system merely stated that they could not handle the unique needs of certain children and excluded them from school. In this respect the regular education did not meet the commitment to educate all children to their potential. Children should not be expelled or excluded from school except under unusual circumstances. Every child should have a legal right to a suitable education. There is no doubt that except in unusual circumstances a child should not miss school for more than a two-week period. Any parent whose child is excluded from school for more than two weeks (and whose child is not hospitalized or very ill) should seek legal aid.

Traditionally the schools in America have assumed educational responsibilities for children from a period beginning at about the age of five or six and ending at about age eighteen. We now know that education at an earlier age would pay rich dividends, especially for the children from the lower socioeconomic levels and other exceptional children, for example, the gifted, the mentally retarded, and the deaf. The CEC policy statement concerning procedure has this to say about educational services at all ages:

> The schools should provide educational services for individuals according to their needs regardless of age. Schools should seek out children who may have specialized educational needs in the first years of their lives. A particular commitment should be made to initiate home care training programs for parents of infants with special needs and kindergarten programs, and specialized components of regular early education programs which serve handicapped children.

The policy drafters state that special education is not different from regular education, but they go on and give a fundamental purpose of special education anyway. It follows:

> The purposes of special educators are not different from those of other educators. The focus is on the individual and his optimal development as a skillful, free, and purposeful person, able to plan and manage his own life and reach his highest potential in society. When special placements are required, the aim still remains that of maximum development and freedom of the individual; to this end, the educational program plays a crucially important role.

Reynolds *et al.* (1971) discuss special education within the schools and the relationships of special and regular school programs. They have this to say:

It is a primary goal of special educators to help build accommodative capacities for exceptional children in mainstream educational programs. It is counted as a gain whenever special educators can assist regular school personnel in becoming resourceful enough to manage the education of exceptional children—either on their own or in team relationships with specialists.

Most special educators would agree that children with special needs should be educated in regular classrooms insofar as this arrangement results in the best education for a particular child. They further state that it is often necessary to remove children from regular classrooms for parts or all of their school programs. And occasionally, most special educators agree, it is necessary to remove some children from their homes and communities for placement in special schools. Some children may go to a resource room for part of their schooling while in the regular mainstream of education and be integrated daily back into the regular classroom. Too often, however, handicapped children are placed in special education classes because they are rejected by regular teachers in regular classrooms and also because they are troublemakers. Too often we see a class of so-called educable mentally retarded who are placed together because they are disruptive to the school system. Very often this defeats the very purpose for which special education was designed.

Reynolds *et al.* (1971) indicate that because special educators deal with children who have unusual needs and unusual school programs they become particularly vulnerable to negative community valuations. Various terms, such as *disability, retarded, disturbed, learning disorders* easily become stigmatic and when attached to children often have unfortunate results. Reynolds *et al.* (1971) state, "Problems are magnified when the field organizes and regulates its program around classification systems which define categories of 'defectives' or 'impaired.'" Sometimes the schemes are more oriented to classification according to etiology, prognosis, or needed medical treatments than to education. At worst simple psychometric thresholds are allowed to become pivotal considerations in educational decision-making.

From the above statement by Reynolds (1971), many special educators know that we have made mistakes in the past when we allowed simple psychometric tests to become a pivotal consideration and also when we allowed a label to control the lives of children. Special education, according to Reynolds (1971), should be defined in terms of the specialized knowledge, competencies, values, and procedures for individualizing instruction as it contributes to all education.

Many special educators resent the labeling process, and they resent the interpretations of their field as it revolves around the labeling process. Many special educators quickly point out that this labeling is an administrative arrangement and that the term *special class* has been and is an administrative term and an administrative arrangement.

Most special educators agree that there is nothing special about special education. What is good for one child is good for all children. Children who have special needs, though, should be served effectively. All people involved in education and all agencies concerned with education should try to help all children be educated to their maximum potential. We should not have regulatory systems which enforce rigid categorization of pupils as a way of placing them in a special class. We should have enough money in a school system to help all children, even if they need specialized programs, without categorizing them. There is no doubt that we have the money in America to help all children. The important thing, though, is where we place the priorities. The special educators argue that we cannot overlook the fact that some children have low intelligence, some children have hearing and vision problems, and many of them are emotionally disturbed. Even though categorizing and labeling of children is indefensible, the fact remains that we must provide services to help these children who do deviate from the norm. Most special educators will tell you quickly that if at all possible these children should remain in the regular classroom, but if they need services outside the regular classroom then of course these services should be provided.

Reynolds (1971) has this to say about the placing of children in special school programs:

> It generally is agreed that children with special needs should
> be educated in regular classrooms and neighborhood schools, insofar

as this arrangement results in good educational progress. However, sometimes it is necessary to provide special supplementary services or to remove children from regular programs for parts or all of their programs. It is necessary to remove some children from their homes and communities for placement in special day or residential schools, hospitals, or training centers. It is desirable that even when residential school placements have been made, some children may be sent to local community schools for parts of their schooling and that the local schools will be fully willing to accept these children. This broad range of programs may be thought of as presenting a general continuum from regular schools to highly specialized schools, often residential, and with this in view, an attitude about placement of children may be expressed.

There is no doubt that the normal home, school, and community life should be maintained whenever feasible for a child who deviates from the norm. Separation of a child from the home should be made only after careful study and for compelling reasons. The last place that a child should be placed is in an institution. After all efforts have failed to help this child, then institutional placement is justified. This does not mean that institutional placement is bad; it is just that separation from the family is so traumatic that this must be a last resort.

Too often, though, as already stated in this chapter, we tend to put handicapped children, particularly, in special facilities because of rejection by regular schools. This is not true of the gifted, and this is why the word *handicapped* was used in the previous sentence. Reynolds (1971) has this to say about this particular subject:

> Unfortunately, it is not uncommon for handicapped children to be put into special education facilities by processes of rejection by regular schools and classes or by simplistic testing-categorizing methods, rather than by careful placement decisions which seek to optimize benefits for the child. When no options exist as so often is the case when planning for both the handicapped and the gifted, or when decisions about children are made poorly, there is denial by education authorities of the fundamental tenet of democratic society and of free public schools. Clearly, the need is to see the school as a whole and in all its parts as a resource for children in which placements are made for valid educational reasons.

Types of Instruction

Reynolds (1962) and Deno (1968) present models of an organizational structure which is an orderly arrangement of service instruction and service strata. This author would like to present a similar arrangement:

1. Exceptional children in the regular classes who get along with regular class accommodations.

2. Exceptional children in the regular classes who must have supplementary services.

3. Exceptional children in regular classes who need modification of materials and procedures.

4. Exceptional children in regular classes who need an itinerant speech clinician, hearing services, or services for the visually handicapped.

5. Exceptional children in the regular classes who spend part of the day in a resource room which is in the same building.

6. Exceptional children in regular classes who spend part of the day having specialized instruction in separate facilities.

7. Exceptional children in special classes.

8. Home-bound instruction.

9. Instruction in hospitals.

10. Institutional placement.

REFERENCES

Council for Exceptional Children: *Exceptional Children, 37,* 1971.

Deno, E.: Educational aspects of minimal brain dysfunction in children. *Proceedings of the Sixth Delaware Conference on the Handicapped Child. Wilmington,* Alfred I. Dupont Institute, 1968.

Reynolds, M. C.: Framework for considering some issues in special education. *Exceptional Children, 28,* 1962.

Reynolds, M. C., *et al.*: Policy statements: call for response. *Exceptional Children, 37,* 1971.

INDEX